50

American Serial Killers You've Probably Never Heard Of

Volume Six

Robert Keller

Please Leave Your Review of This Book At
http://bit.ly/kellerbooks

ISBN-13: 978-1981629442

ISBN-10: 1981629440

© 2017 by Robert Keller

robertkellerauthor.com

Table of Contents

Charles Albright

Prostitute murders are notoriously difficult to solve. So when Mary Lou Pratt's semi-nude body was found in the Oak Cliff neighborhood of Dallas, Texas on December 13, 1990, the police did not have much hope of making an arrest. This murder, however, would turn out to be different. There was nothing unusual about the way Mary Lou had been killed (shot in the head with a .44) but there was something extremely odd about what the killer had done with the corpse afterwards. He had removed both eyes, apparently carrying them away with him.

This gory detail suggested a ritualistic killer, someone who was almost certain to strike again. Dallas PD therefore contacted the FBI, looking for a killer who might have this particular fetish. The search came up empty, and that was particularly unfortunate for 27-year-old Susan Peterson. Her body showed up on February 10, 1991, two months after Mary Lou Pratt had been found. Like Pratt, she was dressed only in a t-shirt and, like Pratt, she had been shot in the back of the head. Her eyes had also been removed.

With confirmation that they were now dealing with a repeat killer, Dallas detectives hit the streets and began questioning the local hookers, at the same time warning them to be vigilant. Those warnings, unfortunately did little good. On March 18, another woman was dead. Unlike the first two victims, Shirley Williams was black. The other details were consistent, though. Williams had been shot and her eyes had been removed.

Three women were now dead and the Dallas police were totally in the dark as to who was responsible. Then, out of the blue, they got a lead. A woman called to suggest her former lover, Charles Albright, as a possible suspect. Asked why she suspected Albright, the woman said that he was a sexual reprobate who had made such weird demands of her that she had ended the relationship. The officer on the other end of the line was just about to thank the caller for the information and hang up when she added another detail. She said that Albright was obsessed with knives... and with eyes.

This, of course, put a totally different spin on things, especially when the police ran Albright through the system and found that he was an ex-con with a lengthy rap sheet. Most of those arrests were for fraud and theft, but there were also charges of assault and sexual molestation of a 9-year-old girl. It was time to bring Charles Albright in for questioning.

In the early hours of March 22, police officers carried out a raid on Albright's residence and took him into custody. Albright, of course, denied all of the charges. The police then carried out a search of his property and found some items that looked promising. These included a red condom similar to one found at one of the crime scenes, a collection of X-Acto knives and a .44 revolver. Unfortunately, none of this was conclusive, especially as the gun turned out not to be the murder weapon. Then Albright's wife provided him with an alibi for all three murders, and it looked like the case was falling apart.

There was still forensic evidence, however. Hairs found on a blanket in Albright's truck was matched to Shirley Williams, and a pubic hair found on Williams's body matched Albright. Then there was testimony from a former friend of Albright, who told investigators that Albright owned a second .44, registered in his father's name. Police were unable to locate the weapon, but the fact that it was missing told its own story.

This was far from the most watertight of cases, but the D.A. decided to file capital murder charges anyway. Those charges were later reduced by a grand jury to second-degree murder, meaning that the death penalty would not be a consideration. The D.A. then decided to drop the Pratt and Peterson cases and to prosecute Albright only for the murder of Shirley Williams. This made perfect sense since Williams was the case for which the prosecution had the most convincing evidence.

Charles Albright went on trial on December 2, 1991. On December 18, the jury deliberated for a full day before returning a guilty verdict. Albright was then sentenced to life in prison, a verdict later upheld on appeal.

FOOTNOTE: The bizarre basis of Charles Albright's eye obsession would later be revealed. As a child, Albright had shared an interest in taxidermy with his adoptive mother. However, they had lacked the funds to buy glass eyes, the most expensive items in the taxidermist's toolkit. The buttons they'd used instead had been a poor substitute. Somehow Albright's fixation had grown from those innocent beginnings.

Paul Bateson

Between the years 1973 and 1978, the city of New York and particularly its gay community was terrorized by a particularly vicious killer. The blood-crazed fiend stalked Manhattan's gay bars, picking up victims, stabbing them to death and them butchering their corpses. In many cases, the remains would be crammed into garbage bags and tossed into the Hudson River, leading NYPD detectives to rather indelicately dub the killings, the "Fag in a Bag Murders."

The first to die was 29-year-old Ronald Cabo who was knifed to death in his West Village apartment on January 4, 1973. The killer then tried to set the apartment alight in an apparent effort to destroy evidence. The fire, however, failed to take hold. Cabo was found where he'd died – butchered on his own couch.

Four days later, 40-year-old Donald MacNiven and John P.W. Beardsley, age fifty-three, were found stabbed to death in

MacNiven's living room at 11 Varick Street. Again an attempt had been made to start a fire but, as yet, the police had not linked the three murders. Neither did they make a connection when the body of gay activist, Robert Borrero, was found bobbing in the Hudson River, just off the Morton Street Pier on January 7, 1973. It was only after a double homicide three weeks later that the NYPD began to suspect that a serial killer may be at work.

On January 28, a Brooklyn Heights building superintendent went to the apartment of 32-year-old schoolteacher Nelson Robert. Other residents in the building had been complaining about a radio that had been blaring at full volume for several hours. Getting no response when he knocked, the super entered using a passkey. He instantly wished he hadn't. Nelson Robert lay on the floor covered by a gray blanket. But even the covering could not hide the blood that had spilled onto the floor. The superintendent ran immediately to call the police. They would find a second corpse in the apartment, this one with his neck snapped. The killer had also killed the couple's pet poodle, drowning the poor animal in the bathtub.

For pure number of victims, the carnage of January 1973 would never be repeated during the reign of the so-called "Bag Killer." But the killing spree was about to make a gruesome twist. From this point on, the killer would dismember his victims and dump them in the city's main waterway. Over the next three years, body parts regularly washed up on the Hudson River piers, a notorious gay cruising spot at that time. Given the state of these remains, the authorities were not able to positively confirm cause of death. They were, however, able to determine how many corpses the parts were from – six in all.

By 1977, the police were no closer to solving the mystery of the butchered bodies, and the gay community was in an uproar. The latest victim, a drag performer named Toni Lee, was strangled to death in her MacDougal Street apartment. Then, on September 14, 1977, the killer claimed his most high-profile victim yet. Addison Verrill was a film critic for Variety magazine and a minor celebrity on the Greenwich Village gay scene. He was found stabbed and bludgeoned to death in his apartment on Horatio Street.

Neither the police nor the New York press initially linked Verrill's murder to the series. But Arthur Bell, editor of the Village Voice, did and published an article decrying the tepid response from both the authorities and the media. That provoked a response that Bell hadn't expected. He received a phone call from a man claiming to be Verrill's killer.

On October 3, Bell published another article, this one entitled "Phone Call from a Fugitive." In it he described his twenty-minute conversation with the purported killer, revealing several details that only the murderer could have known. That elicited another call, this time from a man named Richard Ryan. According to Ryan, the Bag Killer was a man named Paul Bateson. Bateson had apparently boasted to him about the murders when they were in rehab together. After hanging up with Ryan, Bell immediately called the NYPD and gave them Paul Bateson's name.

Bateson turned out to be a 33-year-old former X-ray technician who had fallen on hard times due to drink and drug addictions.

These days, he was reduced to working as an usher at a gay porn theater, and it was there that the police arrested him.

Under interrogation, Bateson quickly confessed to killing Addison. He was less forthcoming, however, about the other murders, and as the police had no evidence against him for those crimes, he would never be charged.

One charge of murder, however, would prove to be enough to put Bateson away for a very long time. Convicted of second-degree murder on March 5, 1979, he drew a term of 20 years to life. Bateson continued to brag about "Fag in a Bag" in prison, saying that he enjoyed killing and that he'd murdered and dismembered his victims "for fun." The other murders remain officially unsolved.

FOOTNOTE: In 1980, director William Friedkin made a movie called *Cruising*, which is loosely based on the case. It later emerged that Paul Bateson had a small part in Friedkin's most famous film, *The Exorcist*.

Daniel Blank

To his colleagues at Airline Motors in LaPlace, Louisiana, Daniel Blank was a good guy, a churchgoing father of four who also happened to be a damn good mechanic. He wasn't the most outgoing or talkative of men, but where was the harm in that? At least he never bad-mouthed anyone. And he never put on airs and graces about his financial success either. Dan Blank was just one of the guys.

The source of Blank's wealth was an open secret within the company. Dan liked to visit the casinos, and he appeared to have the luck of the devil at video poker. His winnings afforded his family a lifestyle way beyond his pay grade. It had financed his recent purchase of a brand new, red Suzuki motorcycle.

During a ten-month period between 1996 and 1997, speculation about Dan Blank's uncanny poker skills had anyway taken the backseat as a topic of discussion. There was a far bigger story in town, a series of six bloody murders, almost all of them targeting elderly residents. The victims had all been killed in their own homes, beaten and stabbed to death. And the motive was quite obviously financial since the properties had all been ransacked. It was also speculated that the killer must be local, since he selected his victims carefully, picking only those who were known to be wealthy.

Which brings us back to Daniel Blank and his barely believable winning streak at the casinos. In retrospect, it might be fair to ask why no one made the connection until an anonymous caller suggested that the police look into it. Detectives then scrambled to check into Blank's backstory and found that he had a juvenile record for arson and had spent time at a reformatory. Since then, he'd stayed mostly on the right side of the law but the police did make an interesting discovery about his gambling activities. Far from being Mr. Lucky, Blank was a serial loser. Wherever his windfall had come from, it wasn't from poker.

That, of course, wasn't enough to arrest Blank on suspicion of murder. But it was enough to invite him down to the Sheriff's office for a friendly chat. Except that Blank, perhaps getting wind of the police inquiries, had skipped town. He'd moved his family to Onalaska, Texas, where he'd set them up in a new double-wide trailer. Then he'd begun negotiations to buy a four-bay automobile repair shop, offering $65,000 in cash. Unfortunately for Blank, he'd never get to complete that transaction. He was arrested in Texas on November 14, 1997, then hauled back to Louisiana to face the music.

Blank made very little effort to deny the murders, confessing almost immediately to six killings between October 1996 and June 1997. Joan Brock, 55, had been stabbed to death in the backyard of her residence in LaPlace; Lillian Philippe, 71, had been savagely beaten with a lamp inside her home in Gonzales. Blank's other victims, Victor Rossi, 41, Barbara Bourgeois, 58, and Sam and Louella Arcuri, 76 and 69 respectively, had all been stabbed and bludgeoned. Another couple, Leonce Millet Jr. and his wife, Joyce, both 66, were shot and beaten but survived the attack. Blank had at least a passing acquaintanceship with all of his victims.

The motive, as suspected, was financial. Blank's gambling addiction had left him broke and desperate, leading him to concoct a terrible plan to make ends meet. All in all, he'd stolen over $200,000 from his victims. The police also learned of the ruses Blank had come up with to convince his family of the source of his newfound wealth. Several times he'd showed up at his father's trailer with one of those oversized checks handed out by casinos to big winners. Except that the checks were fake. Blank never won big. In fact, he hardly ever won at all.

Daniel Blank would face separate trials for each of his six victims. At the first of those, he was found guilty and sentenced to death by lethal injection. That sentence was overturned on appeal and reduced to life without parole. Thereafter, Blank secured plea bargains in the other trials, pleading guilty in exchange for life in prison without parole.

Larry Bright

On a warm summer's day in July 2003, police officers were called to a rural road outside of Tremont, Illinois. A body had been found there, the strangled corpse of an African-American woman, later identified as Sabrina Payne, a 36-year-old prostitute from Peoria, Illinois. Just who had killed her was impossible to say. Prostitution is an extremely perilous occupation, and its practitioners are easy targets for all manner of miscreants. The police did their best with the meager clues they had, but the investigation soon ran out of steam.

Six months later, on February 5, 2004, another body showed up. Like Sabrina Payne, Barbara Williams was African-American, a prostitute and a drug user. Like Payne, she ended up strangled and dumped in a ditch. The investigation, too, followed a familiar path. No clues, no leads, and the considered opinion that one of Williams's johns had killed her, probably in a dispute over drugs or money.

But that theory would be severely tested in the summer and fall of 2004 when, over a three-month period, six more Peoria women disappeared. Two of those women, Linda Neal and Brenda Erving, would be found in similar condition to the earlier two victims. The other four seemed to just vanish into thin air.

The investigation had by now gained a whole new level of intensity. Eight women with a similar victim profile, dead or missing from the same area within a 15-month time frame, pointed to only one thing. A serial killer was preying on the women of Peoria and would likely continue killing unless the police stopped him.

That, however, was easier said than done. The police had hardly any clues, and their appeals for information had met with a muted response. It was only when Peoria and Tazewell counties got together and put up a reward of $20,000 that someone came forward.

Her name was Vicki Bomar, she was a 36-year-old prostitute, and she had a terrifying tale to tell. One night, in August 2004, Vicki had been working her usual beat when a man in a blue pickup stopped to talk to her. He offered her $200 and some crack cocaine in exchange for sex, and so Vicki went with him to his home. Once there, the man produced a knife and ordered her to strip. Then he throttled and beat her into submission and then raped her. He then told her to get dressed, forced her outside and ordered her into his truck. Vicki, however, was convinced that the man intended to kill her. Every instinct told her to run, and so she made a break for it with the man in close pursuit. He was gaining and she was certain that he was going to catch her when she saw the approaching headlights of a car and sprinted into the street towards them. Fortunately for her, the driver stopped, and her assailant then gave up the chase and disappeared into the shadows. Bomar then told the driver she been raped and asked her to give her a ride home. The driver complied. Bomar did not report the incident at the time because she feared that she'd be arrested on some outstanding traffic warrants.

The story was, of course, very interesting to investigators. But one thing about it bothered them. The man that Bomar had described was white. All of the research on serial killers suggests that they prey on victims of their own race and sexual orientation. There are exceptions, of course, but such cases are rare.

Nonetheless, the Peoria police were not exactly swamped with clues. They decided to track down the man, following the scant information that Vicki Bomar had given them. Eventually, in January 2005, they moved in to arrest 39-year-old Larry Bright, an Illinois native who had served two years for burglary. A drug addict who regularly cruised for prostitutes and was known to prefer black women, Bright soon confessed, admitting to eight murders. He also cleared up the mystery of the four women who were still missing. The first four victims had been dumped beside seldom-traveled rural roads; the latter four had been incinerated in a fire pit at Bright's home, their ashes later scattered at various locations.

Larry Bright pleaded guilty at his trial to eight counts of first degree murder. In exchange, the prosecutor agreed not to seek the death penalty. Bright was sentenced to life in prison without parole instead.

Elroy Chester

Between August 1977 and February 1978, the small east Texas town of Port Arthur existed in a state of virtual siege. A murderous burglar was stalking the suburbs, robbing, raping and killing at will with the police apparently unable to do anything about it. Already four people were dead. Seventy-eight-year-old John Henry Sepeda had been shot to death after he encountered an intruder burglarizing his home. Etta Mae Stallings, 87, had suffered a similar fate, killed even as she was reaching for a pistol on her nightstand. And then there was Cheryl DeLeon. In this case, the killer had deliberately stalked the attractive 40-year-old. His intention was to ambush her at her home, tie her up and rape her. But DeLeon fought back, and so the killer cut his losses and executed her in her own driveway.

There had also been a fourth murder in the series but it was different from the others and had not yet been linked by investigators. A 35-year-old man named Albert Bolden had been found shot to death in a vacant house, motive unclear. Unbeknownst to the police, this murder held the key to the entire case. The man who'd shot Bolden was his brother-in-law, Elroy Chester. It was he who had been terrorizing Port Arthur.

Born in Jefferson County, Texas on June 14, 1969, Elroy Chester grew to be an unruly child with learning disabilities. His IQ was tested at just 70, a level that indicates mild mental retardation. Work opportunities were thus few and far between, but Chester didn't need them. After working for a short time as a laborer, he embarked on a career of crime, one that would land him in prison before he turned 20 and keep him there for much of his adult life.

But despite his limited intellectual capacity, Chester was a meticulous planner when it came to committing felonies. He'd wander the streets at night, equipped with his burglary kit of gloves, cutters, ski mask and .380 semi-automatic pistol. When he found a likely target, he'd stake it out, noting who lived there and what their movements were. Before entering the home, he'd cut telephone lines and unscrew outside light bulbs. It was on one of these reconnaissance missions, on the evening of February 6, 1998, that he spotted 17-year-old Erin Ryman and decided to follow her home.

Erin was the unwed mother of a one-year-old, who shared the house with her mother and 14-year-old sister. On this night, however, only she and the baby were at home, perfect for Chester's purposes. After cutting the phone line, he entered through an unlocked side door and confronted the young mother in the living room. Erin had no time to react before he grabbed her by the hair and demanded money and jewelry. He then dragged her through the house, ransacking every room before forcing Erin down to the garage where bound her hands with duct tape. It was at that moment that Erin's sister Claire and her boyfriend Tim entered the home. Their timing could not have been worse.

Dragging Erin back into the house, Chester confronted Claire and Tim and ordered them to submit or he'd blow Erin's head off. Left with no option, the teenagers allowed themselves to be tied up. Then began a prolonged ordeal of sexual assault, during which Erin was raped and both sisters were forced to perform oral sex on Chester. He was just about to rape the younger girl when they all heard a car pull into the drive. The girls' uncle, Billy Ryman, had come to check on them since their mother was working a night shift.

Billy Ryman had barely made it through the door when Chester opened fire on him. Ryman, a Port Arthur firefighter who had received several commendations for bravery, collapsed immediately to the kitchen floor, mortally wounded. Chester then dragged him into the living room where he would bleed to death before help arrived. In the meantime, Chester had fled. But not before firing several shots at Ryman's girlfriend, who was sitting outside in his truck. Fortunately, all of those bullets missed.

Chester was arrested soon after, when investigators finally connected him to the Bolden homicide. Then ballistics provided a link between that and the other murders, and Chester, confronted with the evidence, confessed. He'd committed the murders, he said, because he hated white people. The gun he'd used in the shootings had been stolen from one of his burglary victims.

Chester had by now also been linked to a spate of housebreakings and home invasion rapes.

Elroy Chester was convicted on five counts of first-degree murder in September 1998, with the jury taking just 12 minutes during the sentencing phase to recommend the death penalty. He was executed by lethal injection on June 12, 2013.

Daniel Conahan Jr.

On February 1, 1994, a couple of hunters were scouting a wooded area of Charlotte County, Florida when they spotted buzzards circling overhead. Interested to see what had attracted the scavengers, the men followed the trail and were shocked at what they found. Not the dead hog they'd expected, but a decomposing human corpse. The men immediately left the area and went to call the Sheriff's Department.

The corpse was that of a white male, between 25 and 35 years old. According to the medical examiner, he'd been strangled and had lain in the open for about a month. With no identification, he entered the record as a John Doe.

Almost two years later, on New Year's Day, 1996, Wayne Brown was sitting on his porch in North Port, Florida, when he saw his dog come out of the woods carrying something in her mouth. As the dog got closer, Wayne was horrified to see that she was carrying a human skull. He ran into the house and called the police.

Officers of the Sarasota County Sheriff's Department were soon on the scene. And their search of the surrounding area quickly unearthed the rest of the remains – arm and leg bones, a pelvic bone and a complete rib cage. In this case, decomposition was too advanced for the M.E. to determine cause of death. The corpse became another John Doe.

Two months after that macabre discovery, a man was driving along Route 75 when he felt the call of nature and pulled over to relieve himself. Unfortunately for him, he'd picked a bad place to stop. Just a few feet into the undergrowth lay a nude male corpse. The M.E. would later determine that the victim had been strangled. The killer had then mutilated the corpse, cutting off the genitals and apparently carrying them away with him. And there were similar mutilations to a corpse found on April 16 by two Charlotte County employees. Rope burns around his neck hinted at strangulation and his genitals had been removed.

This latest discovery had investigators spooked since the ritual mutilation of two separate victims pointed to a serial killer. But at least they could put a name to the latest victim. He was 21-year-old Richard Allen Montgomery and he had lengthy rap sheet, with arrests for assault, burglary and grand theft auto.

By now, details of the gruesome discoveries had leaked into the media, and with local papers running lurid headlines about the "Hog Trail Killings," the whole of Charlotte County seemed to be living under a siege. Then, on May 8, the police finally got a break in the case. An inmate at Glades Correctional called them to report an encounter he'd had in March 1995 with a man named Daniel Conahan.

The prisoner's name was David Payton. According to his story, Conahan had picked him up at a Fort Myers bus stop, luring him with the offer of drugs and beer. Once inside the vehicle, Conahan had offered him $100 to pose for nude photographs, which Payton had declined. They'd continued driving, but Payton had become increasingly concerned as they left the city limits and headed deeper and deeper into the woods. Fortunately, the car had become stuck in the mud. They had just freed the vehicle when Payton seized his opportunity, jumped in behind the wheel and sped off, leaving Conahan stranded. Later he'd be arrested for auto theft, for which he was now serving time.

Investigators were at first skeptical of the story, since Payton was known to be a habitual liar. But then two more men came forward with similar tales about a man in a blue Capri, and Daniel Conahan was elevated to the top of the suspect list. Now officers began cross checking police records for similar complaints and soon found one from 1994. A man named Stanley Burden had agreed to pose nude in exchange for $120 offered to him by a white male named "Dan." Dan had driven him into the woods where he'd tied him to a tree under the pretense of taking some "bondage shots." Once he was incapacitated, Dan had sexually assaulted him, then tried to strangle him. Unable to do so, he'd eventually let his captive go, warning him not to report the incident to the police.

Detectives quickly tracked Burden down and confirmed the story with him. Burden even showed them the rope scars on his neck. He was then asked to look at a photo array and he immediately picked out Daniel Conahan Jr. as the man who had attacked him.

Daniel Conahan Jr. was taken into custody on July 3, 1996, and went on trial three years later. On August 17, 1999, he was found guilty of multiple counts of first degree murder and sentenced to death. He currently awaits execution. Since his incarceration, four more corpses have been found, each bearing his unique signature.

Anthony and Nathaniel Cook

During the early eighties, the city of Toledo, Ohio experienced a spate of extremely brutal murders. It started on the night of May 14, 1980, when Thomas Gordon and his girlfriend Sandra Podgorski were sitting in Gordon's Chevy Nova in front of Podgorski's Utica Street residence. Tom and Sandra had just kissed goodnight when the passenger-side window exploded. The couple were then pulled from the vehicle by two burly black men who forced them into the backseat and then drove them to a field in western Lucas County. There, Thomas was shot to death before the men took turns raping his girlfriend. When they were done, one of them stabbed Sandra repeatedly with an icepick, only stopping after she pretended to be dead. Then the men placed Thomas's body in the trunk and threw Sandra in the backseat of the car. The vehicle was later abandoned in North Toledo. After the men left, Sandra was able to stagger to a nearby house for help. The brave young woman would survive her ordeal, but she would bear terrible physical and emotional scars for the rest of her life.

Eight months later, on January 17, 1981, the same two men picked up 19-year-old Connie Thompson as she stood hitchhiking near St. Vincent Medical Center. The teenager's brutalized corpse was later found in a culvert in Lucas County. By the time of that gruesome discovery, the killers had already carried out another attack, gunning down Arnold Coates, 21, and his 18-year-old girlfriend Cheryl Bartlett. Both would survive. The next victim would not be so lucky. Dawn Backes was just 12 years old on February 21, 1981, the day she was snatched from a Toledo street, taken to an abandoned building and there repeatedly raped and tortured before her skull was pulverized with a concrete block.

The police by now had a good idea who they were hunting, thanks to descriptions given by the three surviving victims. But still the killings continued. On March 27, 1981, Scott Moulton, 21, and Denise Siotkowski, 22, were abducted from an apartment parking lot. They were later found stuffed into the trunk of their car, shot to death. Ms. Siotkowski had also been raped. Just over four months later, on August 8, 21-year-olds Stacey Balonek and Daryle Cole met a similar fate, although in this case, the victims were beaten to death with a baseball bat.

On September 18, Todd Sabo and Leslie Sawicki were drinking in their van parked at an apartment complex on Terrace View Drive when they were accosted by a black man carrying a gun. While Sabo struggled with the man, his girlfriend managed to escape, running to the nearest phone booth from which she made two calls, to her father and to the police. Unfortunately, Leslie's father, Peter, arrived at the scene before the cops did. He was shot to death as he got out of his vehicle. Todd Sabo was also shot, but he survived. Soon after the shootings, police arrested a long-haul truck driver named Anthony Cook. Tried and found guilty of murder, Cook was sentenced to fifteen years to life in prison, joining his younger brother, Nathaniel, behind bars. The latter had been convicted on an unrelated charge.

But even back then, the police suspected that the Cook brothers were responsible for many more crimes than the ones they had been locked up for. They just had no way to prove it. Then in 1986 came an important development in forensic detection when a British serial killer named Colin Pitchfork was convicted using DNA matching. The technology still had a long way to go, of course, but in 1997, Toledo investigators were ready to test the Cook brothers' DNA against various cold cases. They soon found a match with the murder of Thomas Gordon and the rape and attempted murder of Sandra Podgorski.

Confronted with evidence linking them to the rape and murder, the Cook brothers decided to cut a deal. In order to avoid the death penalty, they confessed to a total of nine murders, including the 1973 slaying of 22-year-old Vicki Small, one that the police had not linked to them. Anthony Cook had acted alone in this case, offering Vicki a lift after her car broke down, then raping her and shooting her to death. He had been sent to prison soon after on robbery charges and had remained behind bars until 1979. Soon after his release, he and his brother had launched their murderous campaign.

Anthony Cook received an additional life term for the murder of Thomas Gordon. Nathaniel Cook received twenty to seventy-five years behind bars.

Tammy Corbett

When Tammy Corbett was in high school in South St. Louis, Missouri, she was considered a bit of a golden girl. Excellent academically, she also had time to excel at extra-curricular activities, as a cheerleader and as class president. But sometime during her senior year all of that changed. Tammy became more introverted, often surly; her grades fell and classmates sometimes smelled alcohol on her breath. She would later claim that the change came about after she was raped, although no such attack was ever reported. Tammy's version of events also changed with each telling, leading many to conclude that she'd made the whole thing up. This, as we shall see, would become a recurring theme throughout her life.

Whatever her high school travails, Tammy did manage to graduate, although not with the grade average many had expected of her. She didn't attend college, and by 1986, at age nineteen, she was already married, tying the knot with Richard Eveans, whom she'd met through friends a year earlier. Richard must have wondered what he'd gotten himself into when his new bride apparently tried to kill herself on their honeymoon. But things settled down after that. The couple set up home in rural Macoupin County, Illinois. Their first child, Richard Eveans Jr. was born on July 19, 1986. He was followed into the world by his brother Robert a year later.

But this is where the story goes seriously awry. In September 1987, Richard Eveans was away on a work trip when he received a frantic call from his wife telling him that baby Robert had suffered a fall. A few days later, Tammy rushed Robert to the hospital after he supposedly stopped breathing. Doctors ran some tests, found that his lungs were functioning normally and discharged him. But just days later, on September 25, Tammy was back at the hospital, this time carrying a lifeless Robert in her arms. Cause of death was determined to be meningitis, as a result of a small skull fracture suffered in the original fall.

The Eveans family was, of course, devastated by Robert's death. But there was respite from their grief a year later when a daughter Amy arrived. That was on August 16, 1988. Just two weeks later, sixteen-day-old Amy would be dead, her death attributed to Sudden Infant Death Syndrome. That was the second tragedy to befall the Eveans family. The third would not be long in coming.

July 19, 1989, was Richard Eveans Jr's third birthday. It should have been a day of joy, of presents and good wishes for the toddler. Instead, it would end with his tiny body lying on a cold slab at St. Anthony's Hospital in Alton, Illinois. There, the story that Tammy told to explain how her son had died raised eyebrows. She said she was napping with Richard when she had a nightmare about the rape she had endured as a teenager. In the dream, she'd tried to defend herself against the rapist, but she must have physically lashed out because when she woke, she found the toddler lying dead beside her.

With such a wildly unbelievable story and evidence that young Richard had been suffocated, it was hardly a surprise when Tammy was arrested and charged with murder on August 10, 1989. Convicted on that charge, she was sentenced to twenty years in prison, to be served at the Dwight Correctional Center.

But the Tammy Corbett saga wasn't done quite yet. While incarcerated, she decided to come clean about the deaths of her other two children. She had murdered both of them, she said, to get back at her husband. Richard was always traveling for work and she resented him for not paying her more attention. Describing the murders, she said that she had placed her hand over the babies' mouths and noses, suffocating them. "They kicked their legs real hard," she said, "like they were trying to swim." She even managed a chuckle as she recounted that she had killed Amy right beside her husband and he had slept right through it.

Tammy Corbett was charged with the murders of Robert and Amy in April 1991. By then, Richard Eveans had divorced her and she appeared at her trial indicted under her maiden name. On February 5, 1993, she was found guilty but mentally ill. The sentence, nonetheless, was the maximum – life in prison without the possibility of parole.

Scott William Cox

Tia Hicks was missing. Then again, Tia, 20 years old and the mother of two young children, often dropped out of sight. She was a drug user, constantly at war with her demons and sometimes succumbing to their siren song. When that happened, she'd disappear, only to resurface a few days later, remorseful and vowing that it would never happen again.

And so, when Tia disappeared on November 19, 1990, her father, Leonard, was not unduly alarmed. He'd seen it all before and fully expected his daughter to show up sooner or later. This time, however, would be different. A week passed and then another with no sign of Tia. Eventually, on December 13, Leonard Hicks went to a police station in Seattle and reported her missing.

But if Leonard was expecting some sort of urgent response from the authorities, he was to be disappointed. Tia was an adult, she had a drug problem and a habit of dropping out of sight. The report was therefore marked 'unfounded' and filed away. No further action was taken by Seattle PD.

A month after filing his missing person report, an extremely frustrated Leonard Hicks walked into the King County Sheriff's Office and asked to speak to a detective. The one that he got was Tom Jensen, a veteran investigator who had worked the Green River case. And Jensen was more inclined to listen than Seattle PD had been. He immediately got to work, running computer checks, looking for prostitutes and druggies who might have known Tia, contacting the father of her two sons who was currently serving a jail term.

Those inquiries provided Jensen with a long list of names and locations to check out, although none of them got him any closer to learning Tia Hicks's fate. Then, on April 22, 1991, Jensen was scanning police records when something on the screen caught his eye. The Hicks case, formerly "unfounded," had been reopened by the Seattle police. The reason? A nude body had been found inside an old boat that had been left in the parking lot of the Silver Dollar Casino in Mountlake Terrace. The corpse was badly decomposed, but dental work had provided an I.D. The disappearance of Tia Hicks was now a murder investigation.

A month after Tia's body was found, another violent crime was entered into Washington state's Homicide Investigation Tracking System (HITS), in this case, not a murder but an attempted murder. The victim was a prostitute who had been raped, choked and apparently left for dead by her assailant. The woman had later been able to describe her attacker to police – short and strongly built with bushy dark hair and a mustache. She didn't know his name, she said, but she knew that he worked as a truck driver.

This wasn't good news for the investigators. The mobile nature of trucking work makes it the perfect cover for a serial killer. There have, in fact, been a number of high profile serial murder cases involving truckers, Keith Jesperson, Robert Ben Rhoades and Adam Wayne Ford among them. Moreover, the way in which the prostitute had been attacked suggested that she wasn't her assailant's first victim.

So was there another killer trucker stalking the by-ways of Washington? One way to find out was to send out a bulletin to jurisdictions across the state and in neighboring Oregon. The response was almost immediate – two prostitute murders in Portland, Oregon bore the hallmarks of Tia's case.

On November 24, 1990 a woman named Rheena Ann Brunson had been found dead in front of a Safeway store in the city. She had been handcuffed, raped and then stabbed through the heart. Three months later, on February 19, 1991, the partially clothed body of another prostitute, Victoria Rhone, was found inside a railroad car in suburban Portland. She had been strangled.

Unlike in the case of Tia Hicks, the victims were found shortly after they were killed and technicians were able to lift DNA evidence. This provided a match to a man named Scott William Cox, a trucker who worked a route stretching along the west coast from

Canada to Mexico and as far east as Ohio. Cox was brought in for questioning and quickly confessed to killing Brunson and Rhone. He clammed up, however, when asked about Tia Hicks's murder. With no physical evidence, the police were not able to charge him, even though they believe he was responsible. Mountlake Terrace is on one of his routes, and he passed through the town around the time Tia was killed. His course, in fact, took him directly past the Silver Dollar Casino, where her body was found.

Scott William Cox would plead 'no contest' at his trial and accept a jail term of 25 years. He was released on parole in 2013. He remains a suspect in as many as 20 murders, all of which occurred along the routes he worked.

Francisco Del Junco

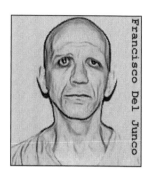

In the early morning hours of Friday, June 3, 1996, a couple of police officers were cruising a Miami, Florida neighborhood when a woman jumped into their path, waving frantically. She explained that she had suffered a brutal beating some nine months earlier and that the police had been unable to find her assailant at the time. "But I just seen him," she blustered, "riding his bicycle like he don't got a care in the world." She then pointed into the darkness. "He went that way," she said.

The officers were somewhat skeptical of this report, since it was quite obvious that the woman was strung out on drugs. But they nonetheless assured the woman that they would keep a lookout for the cyclist. A short while later, and just a few blocks away, they spotted him pedaling his bike along Biscayne Boulevard.

The man was pulled him over and in broken English identified himself as Francisco Del Junco, a 38-year-old Cuban immigrant. His explanation for being out at this hour seemed dubious, as did the bulky rucksack he was carrying on his back. When the officers asked if they could take a look inside the bag, Del Junco readily agreed. It contained a canister of gasoline and a box of matches, and that immediately roused the officers' suspicions. Over the prior six months, there had been a series of gruesome murders in which the victims had been beaten to death and then set on fire. Miami PD currently had a team of 26 officers working the case. Was it possible that this routine stop had netted the serial killer responsible?

There was no way to answer that question just now, but the officers decided nonetheless to take Del Junco into custody. Back at the station, he was handed over to the detectives on duty who decided from the outset on a novel approach to interrogation. Rather than asking the suspect directly about the murders, they engaged him in casual conversation. First they established that he worked as a dishwasher at Dan Marino's American Sports Bar & Grill in Coconut Grove, a job that Del Junco said he "loved." Then they started talking about his childhood in Cuba, his family, his likes and dislikes. Although cagey at first, Del Junco soon opened up and in no time was chatting with the detectives in animated Spanish.

Del Junco would remain in custody for the remainder of the weekend while members of the task force spread out to check on his background. They learned that he had come to America in 1980 during the Mariel boatlift and that he was a loner who seldom contacted the family he had in Miami, had no friends and was not involved in a relationship. At work, he was well-liked and considered a solid, dependable employee who kept to himself and had minimal contact with his co-workers. His arrest record came up clean. Since he'd been in America, Del Junco had not attracted so much as a citation for littering.

So was this meek and apparently harmless little man really Miami's most feared killer? The answer to that question came on Monday, June 6, when Del Junco suddenly asked detectives to take him for a drive. "Listen, I'm going to tell you something," he said. "Can we go somewhere?" He then directed the officers to a spot overlooking Biscayne Bay. There, standing under the palm trees and overlooking the sapphire waters, he started talking.

"You've got to understand," he said. "This wasn't racial. It wasn't about jealousy or revenge and I didn't have sex with these women. It was about relieving tension and that's all I can say." He then went on to admit the murders of four women – Vida Hicks, 43; Diane Nelms, 44; Cheryl Ray, 37; and Janice Cox, 37. All were homeless, black prostitutes who had been killed between August 1995 and March 1996.

"The night you found me," Del Junco continued, "I was going to kill another one. Only this one was going to be much, much worse than the others." He did not elaborate, although several officers later speculated that he intended burning his next victim alive. Fortunately, he'd never get that chance.

Francisco Del Junco was charged with, and later convicted of, four murders. He was sentenced to life in prison in 2002.

Robert Diaz

The story of Robert Diaz is one of the strangest medical serial murder cases ever recorded. Diaz was a vocational nurse who was convicted of murdering 12 patients at a California hospital. That, in itself, is not unusual. Medical serial killers are an all too familiar phenomenon. What makes this case so peculiar is that Diaz claimed to possess psychic powers. He said that he could read the auras of patients and tell whether they would live or die. He could even predict the hour of their deaths. And he was never wrong.

Robert Diaz was born in Indiana in 1938, the thirteenth of sixteen children. He grew up to be a sickly boy who was hospitalized for a significant portion of his childhood. Still, there appeared to be one upside to these long periods under medical care. Robert developed an interest in medicine and told anyone who would listen that he'd one day be a doctor. Unfortunately, his illness meant that he spent long periods away from school, which effectively derailed that ambition. Instead, he dropped out and took a job on an assembly line at an automobile manufacturer.

At 18, a fully recovered Diaz enlisted in the US Marines. But he did not adapt well to military life and within months had gone AWOL, resulting in his eventual discharge from the Corps. Returning to his factory job in Indiana, Diaz again began talking about his ambitions for a medical career. His family and friends, by now accustomed to his grandiose plans, took it all with a pinch of salt.

Something that was less easy to ignore, however, were Robert's bizarre outpourings about the occult. He claimed that he was the reincarnation of an Egyptian Prince and that he had the power to summon demons to do his bidding. He'd spend hours staring at the family cat, convinced that he could gain psychic control over the animal. When he began dating a woman in 1960, he told her that he had summoned her to him using sorcery. Despite this outrageous claim, the woman agreed to marry him the following year and would eventually bear him five children. But the marriage ended in 1972 when Mrs. Diaz tired of her husband's outlandish behavior. Robert then took stock of his life and decided to revisit his earliest ambition. He enrolled on a nursing course and excelled at his studies, graduating near the top of his class. Thereafter, he insisted that family and friends call him Dr. Diaz.

In March 1981, the bespectacled and soft-spoken Diaz began working at the Community Hospital of the Valleys in Perris, California. Shortly after his arrival, there was a significant spike in the rate of deaths at the hospital. Such anomalies are not uncommon, of course, but what worried hospital administrators was that the patients who were dying had apparently been stable just prior to their deaths. And there was something else to concern management. Stories had begun to circulate about the odd behavior of their newest recruit, Robert Diaz. It appeared that Diaz fancied himself as a psychic and had accurately predicted all of the recent deaths.

In April 1981, the San Bernardino coroner received an anonymous tip from a female caller who suggested that the coroner look into the nineteen unexplained deaths that had occurred at Community Hospital in the last month. This tip was passed on to the police and a couple of detectives were dispatched to investigate. Under questioning, an administrator admitted that there were eleven deaths that appeared suspicious. The hospital had been unable to investigate, he said, because the medical records of these patients had disappeared.

That, of course, was a red flag to the detectives. They began questioning nursing staff and soon got to hear of Robert Diaz's prediction game. Several nurses also reported that they'd seen Diaz injecting patients who had later died.

Based on this information, the police obtained a search warrant for Diaz's home and soon uncovered the incriminating evidence they sought. There were vials of the heart drug lidocaine and several syringes, one of them containing 20mm of the drug – a killing dose. Despite protesting his innocence, Robert Diaz was placed under arrest. Now began the unpleasant task of exhuming and autopsying potential victims. Those autopsies showed that twelve of the corpses bore clear signs of lidocaine overdose.

Robert Diaz was indicted on twelve counts of murder in November 1981, after admitting to a grand jury that he had indeed injected patients with lidocaine. He'd done it, he said, in order to provide relief to the patients, after doctors had ignored his pleas for help.

Diaz was still telling this unlikely story when he came before Judge John Hawkins Barnard in April 1984. His defense team had in the interim waived his right to a jury trial which meant Judge Barnard alone would determine his guilt or innocence. The evidence, however, was damning, forging a direct link between Diaz and at least 17 dead patients. No one was particularly surprised when the judge pronounced Diaz guilty and then sentenced him to death.

Robert Diaz was sent to Quentin State Prison to await execution. He died there, of natural causes, on August 9, 2010. He was 72 years old.

Robert Garrow

Robert Francis Garrow was born in Dannemora, New York on March 4, 1936. His father, also named Robert, was a brutal alcoholic who often took out his frustrations on his kids. Robert's mother, Margaret, was even worse. She seemed to revel in cruelty and regularly attacked the children, with Robert the favorite target of her ire. Once she beat him unconscious with a crowbar. On other occasions, her weapon of choice was a brick. In addition, the children received no education and were sent to work on neighboring farms from the age of seven.

These torments continued until Robert was 15 and fought back against his father. Charged with assault, he was sent to reform school, remaining there for a year before joining the Air Force. But military discipline did not agree with Garrow. He was soon arrested for theft and sent to the brig for 18 months. Thereafter, he was given a dishonorable discharge.

Garrow returned to upstate New York, married a girl named Edith and got a job in a fast food restaurant. But he was soon fired after his employer caught him stealing. A year later, in 1961, he was arrested for the rape of a teenaged girl and sentenced to 20 years in prison. He served less than eight years before being released.

Free again, Garrow found work at a bakery and managed to stay out of trouble until 1972, when he was arrested in Syracuse, New York, for abducting two college students. Fortunately for him, the girls refused to testify and the charges were dropped. Then, in 1973, he was arrested for sexually assaulting two pre-teen girls in Geddes, New York. Facing the prospect of a long prison term, he skipped out on his bail and went on the run.

On the morning of July 29, 1973, a group of four friends were camping in Adirondack Park when they were confronted by a gun-wielding Garrow. He marched them into the woods, then tied them to trees, out of sight of one another. Annoyed by the vitriol he was getting from one of the captives, Phil Domblewski, he drew a knife and stabbed the boy to death. He then returned to the other victims but found that two of them had escaped. Garrow then ran to his car and raced away.

The New York State Police launched a massive hunt for the killer, involving hundreds of troopers. But Adirondack Park covers a vast wilderness of 10,000 square miles, and Garrow knew it well. Despite a close run-in with troopers on the night of July 31, he remained at large. By now, the police had discovered a second murder in the park. Twenty-three-year-old Harvard student,

Daniel Porter, had been found stabbed to death. His girlfriend, Susan Petz, 20, was missing.

On August 7, the police got a tip-off that Garrow had visited his sister, Agnes Mandy, in Mineville. They placed the house under surveillance and got their pay-off three days later when Garrow emerged from the woods nearby. A shootout ensued during which Garrow received bullet wounds to his back, legs and hand before surrendering.

Questioned by the authorities, Garrow claimed amnesia regarding the murders and insisted that he knew nothing about the whereabouts of Susan Petz. He told a different story to his lawyers, though, admitting that he'd killed Domblewski, Porter and Petz. He then added a fourth murder, that of Alicia Hauck, a 16-year-old high school student who had gone missing in Syracuse on July 11, 1973. According to Garrow, he'd picked Alicia up hitchhiking, raped her behind a Syracuse apartment building and then stabbed her to death. Her body had been dumped at the Oakwood cemetery. In the case of Susan Petz, he said that he'd kidnapped her after he killed her boyfriend. He'd then spent four days sexually assaulting her before stabbing her to death and dropping her body into an abandoned mine shaft. He even provided detailed directions to the locations of the bodies.

But this information left the attorneys in a quandary. Attorney/client privilege prevented them from telling the authorities, yet there were two grieving families who deserved to know what had happened to their daughters. In the end, they decided that the law required them to keep the information confidential. That decision that would later come back to haunt them.

Robert Garrow went on trial in the Adirondack town of Lake Pleasant on May 9, 1974. His attorneys entering a plea of "not guilty by reason of insanity," but that plea would be rejected by the jury. Found guilty on July 1, Garrow was sentenced to life in prison.

But the story doesn't end there. In September 1978, Garrow tried to escape from the medium-security Fishkill Correctional Facility, using a gun that had been smuggled in by his son. During that attempt, he got into another shootout with the authorities and this time it ended badly for him. Hit three times in the chest, he died on the spot.

FOOTNOTE: The State of New York subsequently attempted to prosecute Garrow's attorneys for not revealing the location of the murdered girls' bodies. Both men were ultimately exonerated, but the controversy destroyed both their reputations and their careers.

Hubert Geralds Jr.

Between 1989 and 1995, there were at least 66 unsolved homicides of women on the mean streets of Chicago's Englewood neighborhood. Many of these victims were full-time prostitutes, while a sizable proportion were women who peddled sex in exchange for drugs, "strawberries" in street parlance. And quite a few of these women fell victim to serial killers, men like Andre Crawford and Geoffrey Griffin, men like Hubert Geralds Jr.

Geralds, like many serial killers, had endured a horrific childhood, during which he was brutalized by a succession of his mother's boyfriends. Perhaps because of those beatings, the boy showed signs of learning disabilities from an early age, with a sub-70 IQ indicating that he was mentally deficient. At his subsequent trial, his defense attorney would claim that he had a mental age of an eight-year-old. Those who knew Geralds better said that he was far from stupid, that he was just knew how to play the system. Playing dumb had got him out of a number of binds. He also used it effectively as a way of luring his victims.

What Geralds lacked in actual intelligence, he made up for in street smarts, and that included devising a way of killing his victims that left no marks on the bodies. Geralds didn't strangle his victims, he suffocated them. This would be achieved by squeezing their noses and applying pressure to their throats – not enough to cause bruises but enough to cut off the air supply. Geralds would then have sex with the victim, fulfilling his peculiar fetish for engaging in intercourse with an inanimate female. Then he'd finish the job and leave the body where he'd committed the murder (usually in an abandoned building).

Because the bodies bore no signs of a physical struggle, the first four of Geralds's murders were attributed to natural causes. But then, Geralds made a mistake. Following his usual routine, he lured a woman to a derelict apartment block, suffocated and raped her, then left her for dead. The woman, however, wasn't dead. She later came around, staggered from the building and went directly to the police. Now the authorities looked at the earlier cases afresh and realized that they had a potential serial killer on their streets.

Then in mid-June 1995, a woman made a call to Chicago PD and reported a gruesome discovery, the decomposing corpse of a woman which had been dumped in a trash can near her home. The woman went further than that, however. She offered the name of the likely killer, her brother Hubert Geralds.

Geralds was arrested soon after. And it wasn't long before he confessed to six murders, even though he denied having sex with the victims and claimed that he'd killed them in disputes over drugs. Whatever the motive, Geralds was booked on six counts of murder. DNA evidence would later link him to four of those victims.

Hubert Geralds went on trial in December 1997. Since he had already confessed and since there was such strong forensic evidence, the defense's only option was to plead mitigation on account of Geralds's impaired intelligence. But the jury chose instead to believe a psychologist brought in by the prosecution. He labeled Geralds a 'malingerer' and said that playing dumb was all part of his M.O. In the end, Geralds was found guilty of all charges and sentenced to death.

But the case of Hubert Geralds had one more twist to offer up. In January 2000, Chicago PD landed an even bigger fish than Geralds, Englewood's most notorious prostitute slayer, Andre Crawford. Crawford would ultimately confess to eleven murders, among them the killing of Rhonda King, a crime for which Geralds had been convicted. So which of these miscreants was telling the truth? The police believed that it was Crawford, since his description of the crime was far more detailed, providing details that only the killer could have known.

Geralds was off the hook for the King murder. But he remained on death row for the other five women he'd killed. That is, until Illinois governor George Ryan commuted all death sentences in January 2003. Hubert Geralds remains behind bars and is unlikely to be released.

Harry Gordon

In the early hours of Saturday, April 6, 1935, a couple walked into a cheap hotel just off the Embarcadero on San Francisco's waterfront. The man was short and stocky with a small, pointy nose and what the clerk would later describe as "sleepy blue eyes." The woman was short and chubby, dark-haired and, like her companion, about mid-thirties. She reeked of cheap perfume. They both reeked of booze. Still, it wasn't the clerk's place to judge. When the man asked for a room and placed a few bills on the counter, he pushed over the register. The man signed it in the name of Mr. and Mrs. H. Myers of San Francisco. Then the couple retired to their allotted room. The clerk glanced at the wall clock in the foyer. It was three a.m.

About two-and-a-half hours later, at around 5:30, the man reappeared in reception and asked the clerk where he could buy sandwiches and some liquor. The clerk told him that he wouldn't be able to buy liquor at this hour but that sandwiches might be purchased at an all-night diner nearby. The man then left the hotel, saying he'd be back soon. He never returned.

By checkout time, the pudgy woman had still not put in an appearance. A maid was sent to rouse her and returned ashen faced and barely able to speak. When the receptionist went up to the room to investigate, he found the woman lying on the blood-drenched bed. She'd been viciously stabbed and beaten, her mouth sealed with adhesive tape to stop her screaming. The coroner would later determine that the wounds had been inflicted with a straight-razor while the victim was still alive. Cause of death, though, was strangulation.

The killer wiped the crime scene of any prints, dashing hopes for a quick arrest. The police did, however, have a solid description of the suspect. He was described as sandy-haired, five-foot-three, 160 pounds. He had a sharp nose and blue eyes set in a pudgy face. The clerk also noted that the suspect had walked with the distinctive rolling gait of a seafarer.

As officers fanned out to search the waterfront, an identification came in on the victim. She was Betty Coffin and she was well known to the police as a prostitute, dope dealer and con artist. Usually, she worked with her husband Ernie, and the police quickly tracked him down to a Gough Street flophouse. However, Ernie was of little help. He had no idea of who might have killed his wife. The murder of Betty Coffin soon turned into a cold case.

On Tuesday, June 25, 1940, San Francisco detectives Ahern and Engler were summoned to the scene of another brutal murder in a downtown hotel. The victim was a petite blonde with a boyish haircut. She'd been strangled and slashed with a razor, which had been left behind by the killer. As in the Coffin case, the scene had been wiped clean of fingerprints.

Questioning the clerk, police learned that the victim (identified as Irene Chandler, a known prostitute) had checked into the hotel at four o'clock the previous afternoon. She'd been accompanied by a man, and his description sounded familiar – short and stocky with a small pointy nose and "sleepy blue eyes."

The police were now convinced that the murderer of Betty Coffin and Irene Chandler was the same man. They also believed that he might be responsible for a series of five unsolved murders committed in San Diego between 1931 and 1934. That prospect gave the investigation renewed urgency as 100 officers were dispatched to waterfront taverns to question staff and customers.

Eight days later, the police caught their first break. A woman claimed that she had seen Irene Chandler in the company of a man named Harry on the day she was killed. She didn't know Harry's last name but said that he was a seaman who had once worked with her husband on a commercial vessel, the Monterey.

Armed with this tenuous clue, Ahern visited the offices of the Matson Line and asked for a list of all sailors named Harry who had worked aboard the Monterey in the last five years. He took that list – numbering 20 – to the Sailor's Union offices and compared it against their records, narrowing the list to eight and then eventually to one – a 35-year-old merchant seaman named Harry W. Gordon, whose description closely matched that of the murder suspect. Further inquiries tracked Gordon to Los Angeles where he was arrested on July 8, 1940, while attending a Sailor's Union meeting.

Gordon initially denied the Coffin and Chandler killings. But he cracked quickly under interrogation and blurted out, "Okay, I killed those girls." Then, to the astonishment of the detectives, he confessed to another murder. "I might as well tell you," he said. "I killed my wife in New York back in 1933."

Inquiries with the New York police determined that Gordon's estranged wife had indeed been murdered and that the case was still open. Florence Gordon had been attacked in her apartment, strangled into submission and then slashed with a razor. The murder, in other words, was startlingly similar to the Coffin and Chandler homicides.

According to Gordon, he'd killed his wife during an argument over child support. But he'd later found that he had a taste for killing, and so he had sought out other victims. He insisted, however, that he'd only killed three women. He knew nothing about the San Diego murders.

Three murders, as it turned out, was enough. Found guilty at trial, Gordon was sentenced to death. He was executed in the gas chamber at San Quentin on September 5, 1941.

Waldo Grant

To the other residents at 7 West 103rd Street, Manhattan, Waldo Grant was the quiet tenant who kept to himself and never caused any bother. He was polite enough, returning greetings in a voice that held a Southern inflection. But aside from the fact that he was from Georgia and had once been married, no one knew a thing about him. They didn't know, for example, that Grant was homosexual. And they most certainly did not know his darkest secret. Waldo Grant was a killer who had murdered four men over the previous four years.

Two of those victims had been killed in the very apartment that the quiet Georgian now occupied; another had been murdered inside an upmarket brownstone on East 124th Street; yet another (the first) had been stabbed and bludgeoned to death at Grant's previous address, 203 West 91st Street. The victim, in that case, had been an 18-year-old named Philip Mitchell.

On September 14, 1973, a resident of the 91st Street apartment building called the police to report a suicide. A young man had apparently flung himself from the roof of the building and now lay dead on the sidewalk. Officers arrived to find the scene as described, except for one thing. A cursory examination of the corpse revealed that this was no suicide. The victim's body bore several stab wounds, and it appeared that he'd also been struck on the head, possibly with an iron bar. Officers therefore fanned out and began knocking on doors. Among those they questioned was

Waldo Grant, who insisted that he did not know the victim and had never seen him before. The case ultimately went unsolved.

Nearly two years later, the body of 23-year-old George Muniz was found inside a metal dumpster on West 91st Street, just a few blocks from where Grant was now living. Muniz had been brutally stabbed, his body bearing numerous knife wounds. With scant evidence, however, the case went cold.

And it was the same with victim number three, a 30-year-old New Yorker named

Harold Phillips. He was found battered to death with a hammer inside his apartment at 27 East 124th Street on October 3, 1976. But the clues again led nowhere and the case file was soon gathering dust. The NYPD certainly had no inkling that the three murders might be connected.

Then, on December 29, a group of children were playing on a footpath in Central Park when they spotted a shopping cart at the side of the path, piled high with several supermarket bags. One of the boys decided to sneak a peek inside a bag and instantly reeled back in horror. A short while later, an officer on patrol was accosted by an excited group of kids. They'd found a body, they said, cut up and stuffed into plastic bags. Half suspecting that he was being pranked, the officer followed the children back to the shopping cart. It only took a single look to confirm that this was real.

The body (later identified as that of 16-year-old Harry Carrillo) had been roughly hacked into three pieces, wrapped in plastic bags and then apparently pushed to the park in the cart. Carrillo had, in fact, already been reported missing. His parents had filed a report after he'd left home to watch a movie on December 26 and had failed to return. So who had killed him? The police started their investigation by contacting the people listed in the teenager's address book. Among those was the name of Waldo Grant.

Grant was brought in for questioning on New Year's Day 1977. Initially, he denied knowing Harry, only changing his tune when detectives showed him the entry in the address book. He then admitted that he'd known the boy for six months but denied that he'd had anything to do with his death.

Unbeknownst to Grant, the police had one solid piece of evidence. Grant had been careless. Among the body parts crammed into the bags, investigators had found a receipt from a supermarket that was in Grant's neighborhood. They'd also been able to lift a clear thumbprint from it. Now they asked Grant if he'd provide a set of prints for comparison. Faced with that evidence, Grant finally broke down and confessed, admitting also to the other three murders. In each of the cases, he'd been overcome by "an uncontrollable urge to kill," he said. He'd been unable to stop himself.

Waldo Grant was convicted of three counts of murder in 1977. He was sentenced to life in prison.

Kenneth Granviel

It was one of the bloodiest crime scenes that investigators in Tarrant County, Texas had ever seen. On October 7, 1974, police units were called to an apartment complex in Fort Worth. There they found the butchered corpses of three women and two children, one of them a little girl just two years old. All of the victims were members of the McClendon family, and whoever had killed them had acted with extreme cruelty. The victims had been tied up, brutally raped over an extended period, and then systematically slaughtered. The killer had then fled the scene, leaving behind a bloodbath that resembled something out of a horror movie.

The Fort Worth Police were quite obviously keen to apprehend the perpetrator of this outrage, not least because a killer who acted with such depravity was very likely to reoffend. But despite the frenzied nature of the crime, the perpetrator had left few clues. Those that were left behind were checked out, of course, but they led investigators down one dead end after the other. Despite early optimism, the trail soon ran cold. All the police could do now was to wait and hope. Wait until the killer slipped up and hope that that slip came before he killed anyone else.

Five months passed. Then, on February 8, 1975, a man named Kenneth Granviel walked into a Fort Worth police station accompanied by a pastor. He said that he wanted to speak to a detective and, during the subsequent interview, admitted to seven murders and five rapes. He then asked detectives to drive him to an apartment in Fort Worth where they found another family who he had been taken hostage. The women had been tied up in a similar fashion to the McClendons. One had already been raped. It appeared that Granviel had then broken off the attack, walked to a local church and asked the pastor to go with him to the police so that he could give himself up.

Back at the station, the suspect reduced his oral confession to writing. He was Kenneth Granviel, an unemployed machinist who had lived his entire life in Fort Worth. He said that he was a friend of the McClendon family and had been particularly fond of his youngest victim, 2-year-old Natasha. That, however, had not stopped him from killing the toddler. "I could see it happening," he said. "I could see myself stabbing this little girl who I used to play with, who I used to buy candy for. There was nothing I could do about it."

And the McClendons were not Granviel's only victims. He also confessed to raping and killing two female acquaintances and burying their bodies. Later, he'd lead police to recover the decomposed remains of the victims who had both been raped and then savagely stabbed to death.

Granviel had now confessed to seven murders, but he would stand trial for only one, that of 2-year-old Natasha. His trial began in March of 1983, with the defense arguing that he should not be eligible for the death penalty due to mental incompetence. Given the horrific testimony presented at trial and the tender age of the victim, that was never likely to succeed. On May 5, 1983, having already found Granviel guilty, the same jury returned with the recommendation that he should be put to death.

Kenneth Granviel was due to be the first inmate put to death by lethal injection in the United States, but legal wrangling delayed his execution by 21 years. By the time he eventually kept his date with the executioner on February 27, 1996, he was the longest-serving inmate on death row at the Huntsville Unit. Granviel declined to give a final statement. He was pronounced dead at 6:20 p.m., eight minutes after the lethal drugs began flowing into his veins.

Geoffrey Griffin

Prostitution is a dangerous game, one which requires its practitioners to get into cars with complete strangers, who drive them to isolated spots, to hope that the exchange of sex for cash goes smoothly and that they come to no harm. But, of course, that is not always the case. Many women end up robbed, raped, beaten and slashed by their "dates" with very little recourse to the law. Some even end up dead.

Yet, even in this murky netherworld, few women can have been as badly afflicted as the streetwalkers of Chicago around the turn of the 21st century. This was a time during which a number of serial killers were active on the city's Southside, and abandoned buildings were littered with brutalized corpses. The police might have thought they'd stemmed the tide with the arrest of Andre Crawford in January 2000, but no sooner did they have Crawford under lock and key than another monster appeared on the scene. And he seemed determined to challenge Crawford for the title of the area's most prolific killer.

On May 2, 2000, a 33-year-old woman was found raped and strangled to death inside an abandoned building on the 15800 block of South Park. Ten days later, a 32-year old woman was found in similar circumstances, this time in a building on South Yale. Five days after that, there was a third corpse, this one both strangled and bludgeoned.

The rape kit performed on all of these victims had produced a DNA sample, and the police were confident that they'd make an arrest as soon as the results were back from the lab. After all, someone who killed in such a brutal, yet organized way, was not a first-timer. He must have a record. Unfortunately, that was not the case. DNA proved that the same man was responsible for all three murders, but there was no match on the state database.

Then, on June 13, 2000, came a potential break in the case. A 21-year-old woman was lured to an abandoned building on South Wallace Street with the promise of sharing some drugs. Once there, her male companion drew a knife and attempted to rape her. The woman, however, was able to rake her nails across the attacker's face and break free. She ran naked from the building. Later, she'd describe her assailant to police as a powerfully-built black man in his late twenties or early thirties. That was hardly much help, but the skin under her fingernails did provide a DNA match. It was the same man who had committed the three murders.

And soon three would be four. On June 16, 2000, a 29-year-old woman was found beaten and strangled to death in a building on South Michigan. Three days later, another body was found, this one significantly decomposed with an estimated date of death about a month earlier. And the death toll kept mounting with two more corpses discovered over the next week. All were linked by DNA to the same man. Within the space of just over a month, the so-called "Roseland Killer" had committed a staggering seven murders. At the rate he was going, he would soon be ranked among America's most prolific serial killers.

Chicago PD had to do something fast, and so they leaned hard on their snitches and soon unearthed a clue. A man named Geoffrey Griffin had been seen in the company of Angela Jones, one of the victims, on the day she died. According to the informant, Griffin was a crack cocaine user who often went with prostitutes. He also matched the rather vague description given by the surviving victim.

It seemed tenuous at best, but with nothing else to go on, the police decided to bring Griffin in for questioning. To their surprise, he admitted almost immediately to killing Jones, although he claimed it had been accidental. According to him, he'd "squeezed her throat" during sex and she had "stopped breathing."

Geoffrey Griffin was charged with one count of murder. A search warrant was then served at his residence and turned up a jacket with blood spatters on it. That blood was matched to Beverly Burns, another of the Roseland Killer's victims. Griffin was also linked via DNA to all of the dead women.

Griffin, however, would stand trial for only two murders, those of Angela Jones and Beverly Burns. In the Burns case, a judge decided to acquit, accepting Griffin's explanation that Burns had suffered a nosebleed while they were together. In the Jones murder, the one that he claimed was accidental, he was found guilty and sentenced to 100 years in prison. DNA has since linked him to a series of rapes and to another murder, committed in 1998.

William Guatney

William Guatney was 57 years old and he'd been riding the rails, travelling the length and breadth of America, for four decades. In popular parlance, he was a bum, except you wouldn't want to call him that. The word served as a red rag to the normally affable Gautney, and when he was angry, he could be mean, very mean indeed.

Still, Guatney seldom lost his temper. Friends described him as a "happy-go-lucky type of guy." He'd breeze into town on a freight train, usually when there was a state or county fair on. There, he'd offer his services to stockmen, caring for their cattle and keeping the stalls clean. He was well-liked by his employers because he was a hard worker and usually of an upbeat disposition. He was also popular with children, seeming to have an uncanny rapport with them. Often, there'd be a crowd of giggling kids around the stalls where he worked, urging him to do his famous impression of a steam train whistle. When he obliged, there'd be peals of laughter. This party piece earned him the nickname "Freight Train." He also went by another name, "the Pied Piper of the Fairgrounds."

On the surface, that name appears innocent enough, charming even. But when you look at it from another angle, it takes on a far more sinister connotation. William "Freight Train" Guatney's interest in children was not as innocent as it may have seemed. He was a pedophile with a particular interest in little boys. In fact, although it went unnoticed at first, there was a worrying trend associated with Guatney. In towns where he worked, children often went missing. Some would later be found, raped, beaten and stomped to death. Others simply disappeared forever, as though the earth had swallowed them up. Between the years 1974 and 1979 alone, there were fifteen such cases.

In July 1979, police officers from Illinois, Nebraska, Iowa, Kansas, Arizona and California got together to form a task force. Their focus was a series of murders involving young boys, all of them committed in towns that lay on the rail network and had recently hosted a town or county fair. It was an officer from Lincoln, Nebraska who first named Guatney as a suspect and once the name was out there, it made perfect sense. Guatney was a common denominator, riding into town on the rails, doing his stint at the fair, and then riding out again, often with a murdered child left in his wake.

A massive hunt was now launched for the traveling hobo, a search that ended two months later, in August 1979, when Guatney was pulled from a train in Illinois and arrested. He was initially charged with the murders of 13-year-old Jon Simpson and 12-year-old Jacob Surber, who had gone missing from the state fair in Lincoln, Nebraska in 1975. The boys' battered corpses had been found days later. Both had been sodomized and had suffered a severe beating before being strangled to death.

To those two charges was soon added another, this one from Topeka, Kansas. Twelve-year-old Jack Hanrahan had disappeared from his Topeka neighborhood on May 20, 1979. His corpse, found ten days later in a creek bed, bore all the familiar signs. The child had been raped, beaten and stomped before his life was ended by a powerful pair of hands pressing down on his throat. The Topeka Police thought "Freight Train" was responsible while officers in at least ten other jurisdictions believed that they had enough evidence to pin their unsolved child killings on him.

But Guatney was being held in Illinois and was unlikely to be extradited before that state had brought him before its courts. On August 20, he was charged with the first-degree murder, kidnapping and sodomy of 9-year-old Mark Helmig, killed at Pekin, Illinois in 1976. There were also charges relating to the murder of 14-year-old Marty Lancaster, killed in the town of Normal, Illinois in 1978.

William Guatney was brought to trial in Illinois in 1980. He refused to enter a plea and despite a tape-recorded confession to the two murders, he was ruled incompetent to stand trial and committed to a mental institution. He died there in 1997 taking his secrets with him to the grave. He remains a suspect in countless child murders.

William Inmon

In September 2009, a somewhat disheveled young man walked into the police station in Springerville, Arizona and demanded to speak to Police Chief Steve West. The man, 21-year-old William Inmon, had a strange complaint. He told the Chief that officers from the nearby town of St. Johns had arrived at his apartment with a search warrant. He wanted to know if West was going to run them out of town for encroaching on his jurisdiction.

West, of course, was going to do nothing of the sort. He knew why the St. Johns officers were there. Inmon had been implicated in a murder, the shotgun death of a 16-year-old named Ricky Flores. He therefore told Inmon to calm down, offered him a cup of coffee and invited him to take a seat in his office. Then he started chatting to the young man, keeping things casual and friendly. Before long, Inmon had opened up to him, talking about his childhood in south Phoenix where he claimed that he was often left to fend for himself because his parents were either drugged up or in jail. Over the next four hours, the veteran officer skillfully guided the conversation, with Inmon talking openly about his political views, stating that he believed society would be better off without certain "undesirables." Then finally, he admitted that the St. Johns officers had just cause for searching his home. He had indeed been involved in the Flores shooting.

According to Inmon, he'd killed Flores at the behest of Jeffrey Johnson, the father of Flores's girlfriend. Johnson was unhappy about his daughter's relationship with the drug-addicted 16-year-old, by whom she already had a child. He'd asked Inmon to take care of Flores, and Inmon had had no problem carrying out the hit. Flores was, after all, the exact type of person that Inmon wanted removed from society.

But whatever Inmon's views on who deserved to live or die, homicide was still a crime in the state of Arizona. He was booked for the murder of Ricky Flores and taken into custody. And he wasn't done confessing yet. Within two weeks of his incarceration, he'd admit to two more murders.

The first of those came in April 2007, when he shot 72-year-old William "Stoney" McCarragher to death. McCarragher was a bit of a local character, known for his gruff demeanor and reputed to have large amounts of cash stashed at his ranch. He often hired local teens to do odd jobs around his property but, according to Inmon, his real interest in them was sexual. He claimed that he'd done some research on the old man and found that he was a convicted pedophile with a lengthy record of sexual offenses under his real name.

The final straw had come when McCarragher had hired him to do a job on the ranch and then touched him inappropriately. That was when Inmon decided that he had to die. That same night, he'd crept up to McCarragher's ranch house carrying a shotgun. Spotting his quarry through a window, he'd raised his weapon and fired, severely injuring the old man. He'd then entered the house and finished McCarragher off. He'd done it, he said, so that McCarragher couldn't hurt anyone else.

Inman's next victim was a deaf Vietnam veteran named Dan Achten, known locally as "Hummer Dan" because of his constant, tuneless humming. Achten had been found shot to death and buried in a shallow grave near his home early in 2009. Now Inmon was admitting that he was the shooter. According to him, Achten was a drug addict who "generally mistreated people." But he'd only decided to kill Achten, after Achten shot his dog.

Inman also admitted that there were others on his hit list marked for death and that he would have continued killing had he not been caught. Like all missionary serial killers, he insisted that he was doing society a favor by getting rid of "undesirables." His mission would cost him a 24-year prison term, after he entered a plea bargain with prosecutors.

Elton Manning Jackson

Over the span of ten years, from 1987 to 1996, the gay community of Portsmouth, Virginia lived in dread of a fearsome serial killer. The so-called "Hampton Roads Killer" preyed on drifters, transients and hustlers, racking up a death toll of eleven victims, all of them homosexual. Yet there was one thing about the victims that confused the police. Some were black and others white, and since serial killers typically prey on their own race, investigators were left to wonder. Were they dealing with one perpetrator or two?

The signature of the killer suggested the former. The victims were invariably picked up in Portsmouth and dumped in Chesapeake, always near on-ramps to interstate highways. All of them had been strangled, some manually, others with a ligature. All were known to have frequented gay bars or places where men seek out other men for sex. That, in turn, put another obstacle in the path of investigators. The gay community simply did not trust the cops and were reluctant to share information.

Then, on July 22, 1996, there was a 12th murder. The body of Andre Smith was found beside a roadside, apparently strangled to death. An autopsy would later confirm that to be the case and also put the time of death at around 18 to 24 hours before the discovery of the corpse. That, in turn, provided detectives with a time frame to work with, and they soon had confirmation of the victim's movements during his final hours. A friend of Smith's came forward to say that he had been with him on the evening prior to his death. Smith had told him that he was going to collect some money from a man named Elton Jackson and would be back soon. He had never returned.

This was a promising lead, and the detectives soon tracked down Jackson and asked if he would answer some questions. Jackson agreed but then surprised investigators by insisting that he didn't know anyone named Andre Smith. That in itself was suspicious but Jackson further aroused suspicion with his demeanor. He was fidgety and tentative, refusing to make eye contact with his questioners. That, however, was not reason enough to arrest him, and the detectives eventually left frustrated.

The murder of Andre Smith would remain unresolved over the next ten months. But the police were far from idle during that time. They were compiling a profile of their killer and processing DNA evidence lifted from the victim's body. Eventually, on May 6, 1997, they felt they had enough to charge Elton Jackson.

Jackson was taken into custody that same day and he now offered a markedly different story. He now said that he *had* known Andre Smith and admitted that they had been together on the night Smith died. He'd lied earlier, he said, because he did not want to admit to being gay. He said that he and Smith had engaged in sex at his house on the night in question but insisted that Smith had left straight after. He'd likely encountered his killer later that night, Jackson suggested.

That was exactly the story that the police had expected Jackson to tell and they were ready for it. Had Smith been inside Jackson's car on the night of the murder, they wanted to know. Jackson said that he hadn't. How then had fibers from the car's carpet ended up on Smith's body? How had Smith's DNA ended up on cigarettes butts found in the vehicle? Had Smith been in Jackson's bed? Again Jackson said no. How then had a speck of his blood ended up on the bed sheets? Jackson could provide no explanation and was therefore arrested on suspicion of murder. He would later be tried, found guilty, and sentenced to life in prison.

But what of the other Hampton Road murders? How can we know that Jackson committed those? Well, Jackson has never been charged with those murders, so technically they remain unsolved. Portsmouth police have, however, closed their files believing that the perpetrator is already behind bars and will never be released. How can they be so sure? Because the signature is consistent across all twelve homicides, pointing to a single perpetrator. There is also DNA evidence linking Jackson to some of the victims. Most of that was obtained from semen lifted from the corpses, but in the cases of Andre Smith and another victim, Reginald Joyner, there were flecks of blood found on Jackson's bed sheets. It all points to Elton Jackson being the Hampton Roads Killer. Perhaps most tellingly, there were no further murders after his arrest.

Vickie Dawn Jackson

The town of Nocona, Texas is a tiny, rural burg in the north of the Lone Star state, population just over 3,000. Its hospital, Nocona General, is correspondingly small with a capacity of just 45 beds. Yet, over a period of two months, between December 2000 and February 2001, occupying one of those beds must have seemed like a death sentence. During that short span, a total of 22 patients died at the hospital.

At first, hospital administrators thought that they were just experiencing a run of bad luck, as can happen at any medical facility. But then, on February 6, 2001, several vials of the drug Mivacron were reported missing from the hospital's inventory. This medication is used to temporarily stop a patient's breathing so that a tube can be inserted into the lungs. It can be lethal if administered incorrectly or with bad intentions, and the hospital therefore alerted the police. The subsequent inquiry would lead investigators to a shocking conclusion. There was a serial killer working the wards of the tiny hospital, a licensed vocational nurse by the name of Vickie Dawn Jackson.

Vickie Dawn Jackson was born in Indiana and moved with her parents to Nocona when she was still a baby. She grew up in the town and as a teenager fell pregnant by a local boy who she later married. That marriage soon ended in divorce, and before she was twenty, Jackson was pregnant again, this time by a man named Leroy Carson. Jackson had never intended marrying Carson, but she went through with it for the sake of her unborn child. Her son was born soon after the nuptials, and thereafter Jackson fell pregnant again, this time giving birth to a daughter, Jennifer, in 1984. Just 18 years old, Vickie was now the twice- married mother of three young children.

But she wasn't about to give up on a long-held ambition. Since high school she'd been telling anyone who would listen that she wanted to be a nurse. Now, with her children still in diapers, she began attending night classes, graduating a year later with an LVN qualification. Thereafter, she worked at several medical facilities in the area, never staying too long at one job, always quitting after a short time over one or other grievance. Despite insisting that nursing was her passion, Vickie spent an inordinate amount of time complaining about her colleagues and patients.

She was no picnic at home either. Both her husband and children had to endure her rants and bad moods, and she often attacked her children physically. Eventually, after 12 years of marriage, Leroy Carson opted out. He divorced his wife in 1996. Wasting no time, Vickie soon married for a third time, tying the knot with Kirk Jackson.

Fast forward to 2000 and Vickie Dawn Jackson's life was in tatters. That was the year that she lost custody of her children, who had complained of abuse by their stepfather. It was also the year that she suffered a miscarriage, after falling during a physical altercation with her husband. And it was the year that Jackson visited a psychiatrist and was diagnosed as bipolar.

Another significant event occurred in 2000; Jackson started working the night shift at Nocona General Hospital and, soon after, patients started dying. Now, after the report of missing vials of Mivacron, the police were brought in and uncovered a startling discrepancy. Of the 22 patients who had died at the hospital in recent months, 21 had perished on the night shift. And few of those patients had been seriously ill. One was being treated for a foot injury, another for diarrhea, a third was an elderly man with dementia who was otherwise in good health.

Had these patients been deliberately killed by someone on the hospital staff? Detectives feared so, and their investigations led them eventually to Vickie Dawn Jackson, the only person who had been on duty at the time of all the deaths. Then a search warrant was obtained for Jackson's home and turned up a used syringe which contained traces of Mivacron. That resulted in an exhumation order being granted on ten patients who had died under suspicious circumstances. Each of their bodies tested positive for traces of mivacurium chloride.

Vickie Dawn Jackson was arrested in July 2002 and indicted on ten counts of murder. However, it would be four years before the matter came before the courts. When it did, she pleaded "no contest" and accepted a term of life in prison without parole. Since Jackson refuses to discuss the case, we will never know her motive for taking so many innocent lives.

James Allen Kinney

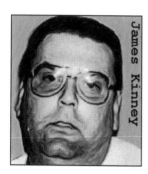

Keri Lynn Sherlock was 20 years old and she was keen to see the world. The Braintree, Massachusetts resident had hardly been out of her home state on the day, in 1988, when she got on board a Greyhound bus bound for Bellingham, Washington. Keri had an uncle there, and she was interested in checking out the study opportunities available at Western Washington University. She also wanted to see the Pacific Ocean for the first time.

But Keri Sherlock would find something far less agreeable in the Pacific Northwest. She would find a man named James Allen Kinney while she was out one day hiking in the woods. She would end up savagely raped and beaten to death, her body dumped along a lonely stretch of blacktop on the Mount Baker Highway. A backpack found near the crime scene quickly linked Kinney to the murder, but by the time officers came to arrest him, Kinney had already fled. He would remain at large for three years.

James Allen Kinney was born Earle Suskey in Tulsa, Oklahoma on September 5, 1949. His father was a violent alcoholic who would abandon his family often, sometimes for months at a time. That, inevitably, tore the family apart, and by the time he was two years old, Earle and his younger brother, Robert, were in foster care. Later, a young couple, Margaret and Clifford Kinney, would formally adopt them and Earle Suskey would become James Allen Kinney. Shortly thereafter, the family moved to Lansing, Michigan, so that the boys could grow up on a farm.

It sounds idyllic, and to an extent it was. James joined the Boy Scouts and he raised his own cows, earning a badge from the Future Farmers of America. Clifford often took them fishing. On the other hand, there was Margaret, a stern, God-fearing woman who believed in the credo, "spare the rod and spoil the child." From her, there was very little affection but plenty of punishment. On one occasion, she took a horse whip to James, leaving him with a permanent scar across his right cheek. Little wonder, then, that he took the first opportunity to leave home, joining the US Army in 1967 and shipping out to Vietnam.

By the time Kinney returned from southeast Asia in the early 1970s, he was showing signs of the mental problems that would continue to plague him for the rest of his life. During the seventies and early eighties, he would be committed for extended psychiatric treatment on at least 26 occasions. During those hospital stays, he would be diagnosed with various conditions, including paranoid schizophrenic, bipolar disorder and post-traumatic stress disorder.

Despite this, Kinney would always be discharged eventually. And when he was at liberty, he traveled. Coast to coast and from the Great Lakes to the Deep South, he roamed, living off his disability checks and crashing at homeless shelters and VA hospitals. It was during this time, investigators believe, that he started killing.

Exactly how many victims Kinney is responsible for is unknown, although he has been definitely linked to the 1997 murder of Billie Jo Watson in Grand Rapids, Michigan, and to the death of another woman in Des Moines, Iowa, a year later. Watson was last seen alive on the night of November 30, 1997, accompanied by a man matching Kinney's description. Four days after her death, Kinney bought a one-way bus ticket out of town, abandoning a business he'd started and leaving behind all of his personal belongings. In addition to these two murders, there was also evidence linking Kinney to homicides in Virginia, Minnesota, Ohio, Idaho and Oregon.

Now, though, Kinney was in hiding and not even the efforts of the FBI, which had elevated him onto its *Ten Most Wanted* list, could uncover his whereabouts. It was only after his case was featured on the television program *America's Most Wanted* that a lead emerged. A viewer in North Carolina called in to say that he recognized Kinney. The fugitive was arrested a few days later at Philadelphia International Airport as he waited to board a flight. He had almost evaded his pursuers again.

Kinney was taken back to Washington where he readily confessed to the murder of Keri Lynn Sherlock. According to Kinney, he'd picked her up hiking, driven her into the woods and raped her before beating her to death. He made no mention of the postmortem mutilations inflicted on the body, a feature of many of his crimes.

James Allen Kinney was tried for the murder of Keri Sherlock in January 2002. He entered a guilty plea and was sentenced to life in prison without parole. To date no other state has sought to indict him.

Anthony Joe Larette Jr.

At around 11:00 a.m. on the morning of Friday, July 25, 1980, a couple living in an apartment block in St. Charles, Missouri were startled by someone banging at their front door. The man went to answer it and got an even bigger shock. Their neighbor, 18-year-old Mary Fleming, lay collapsed on the doorstep. Mary was naked, save for a bikini top and she was bleeding profusely from a neck wound. She had also been stabbed several times. The neighbor shouted back into the apartment for his wife to call 911. Then, as he crouched down to assist the badly injured teen, he saw a man dash from the Fleming apartment and run down the stairs. Moments later, another resident of the apartment building saw the same man sprint across the car park, jump into a cream-colored convertible and speed away, leaving rubber on the tarmac. By then, police units and an ambulance were already on their way.

Mary Fleming was rushed to a local hospital where she was found to have suffered numerous injuries, including cuts, bruises and several stab wounds. The most serious, though, was a deep slash that ran from ear-to-ear severing major veins and arteries on its path. The blood loss was profuse, and despite the valiant efforts of ER personnel, Mary didn't make it. The subsequent autopsy would reveal that she had never stood a change. One of the chest wounds had collapsed a lung, another had penetrated her heart. So savage was the attack that the tip of the blade had broken off and was found inside the abdominal cavity. This was now a murder investigation.

As detectives surveyed the blood-spattered residence, they learned the tragic circumstances of the murder. Mary, a recent high school graduate, should not even have been home that day, but she'd cried off her summer job with a migraine. The police also received their first lead, and it was a solid one. The resident who had seen the man jump into his car and drive away had had the presence of mind to jot down the license plate number. Running the plate, investigators learned that the car belonged to a man named Richard Roberson.

Roberson was easy to find, and he provided the police with the next piece of the puzzle. He said that he'd loaned his car that day to a friend named Tony Larette, to enable Larette to attend an interview. Officers then asked him to describe Larette and he did, providing a description that closely matched the man seen running from the crime scene.

As any homicide detective will tell you, the first 48 hours of an investigation are the most critical, with the prospects of making an arrest diminishing rapidly from then on. Now, 48 hours in, the St. Charles police already had a strong suspect. The problem was that

that suspect was nowhere to be found. He'd hopped a Greyhound out of town, destination, Topeka, Kansas.

This, of course, complicated matters. But, at least, Richard Robeson was prepared to help. With officers listening in, he called his friend at the home of his family in Kansas. Robeson told Larette that he'd found blood in his car and demanded an explanation. Larette then admitted that he'd killed a woman while committing a burglary. The only motive he offered was that the woman had started screaming after he'd told her not to. It was enough for Missouri police to ask their Kansas colleagues to take Larette into custody.

St. Charles police initially interviewed Larette at the Shawnee County lockup in Topeka. Initially, he claimed that he'd picked up a hitchhiker and that it was the hitchhiker who'd killed Mary. By the following day, however, he was ready to admit that it was he who had killed Mary Fleming, offering the same motivation that he'd given Robeson. "I warned her to be quiet," he said, as if that justified everything.

Larette would ultimately be convicted of the murder of Mary Fleming and sentenced to death. He went to meet his maker, via lethal injection, on November 29, 1995. But not before he did a whole lot of talking. While on Death Row, he frequently spoke to detectives, admitting to 50 rapes and at least a dozen murders. According to Larette, he'd spent fourteen years traveling the country by bus, stopping off wherever the mood took him. During that time, he'd committed murders in Arkansas, Colorado, Illinois, Louisiana, Mississippi, Nebraska, Texas, Virginia, Florida and Kansas.

Of course, many inmates boast about murders they did not
commit. But in Larette's case, many of the details checked out. He
was definitively linked to at least two murders besides Mary
Fleming. One of those was of a 26-year-old woman named Tracey
Miller, who he killed in 1978 in circumstances that were
startlingly similar to the Fleming murder. Just what Anthony Joe
Larette's final death toll was, we shall never know.

Gerald Patrick Lewis

Gerald Patrick Lewis was born in Jacksonville, Florida, on August 10, 1965. He was raised in a comfortable, if shiftless, middle-class environment with his family making several moves between Georgia and Massachusetts. As a result, Gerald formed no close friendships in childhood. He did, however, display a number of aberrant behaviors. He was a fire-starter, a tormentor of animals, and a chronic bed wetter. These three behaviors, known as the MacDonald Triad, are often found in the histories of serial killers.

Dropping out of school in the ninth grade, Lewis started drinking heavily and using drugs, supporting his addictions through burglary. That eventually landed him in prison, first for a six-month stretch and then for four years, of which he served barely half. Moving to Weymouth, Massachusetts after this latest release, he got a job as fryer at a Kentucky Fried Chicken and started dating fellow employee, Lena Santarpio. Soon Lena was pregnant was his child.

Lena's parents were less than happy about their 16-year-old daughter's ex-con boyfriend. But they were determined to do the best for their grandchild, and so they invited Lewis to live in their home. But life in the Santarpio household was far from easy for Lewis. Lena's parents were constantly on his case, and to make matters worse, Lena stopped having sex with him as her pregnancy progressed. In revenge, Lewis took to cruising for prostitutes. Then, one August night in 1986, he picked up a woman from a bus stop and raped her at knifepoint.

Lewis was arrested soon after. By the time he emerged on bail three months later, Lena had already given birth and wanted nothing to do with him. Distraught at this rejection, Lewis started stalking Lena, begging for another chance. It was to no avail. Lena never spoke to him again and he never got to see his son. That, perhaps, was the driving force behind the murder spree to come.

The first murder attributed to Gerald Patrick Lewis occurred just before Christmas 1986. The victim was a hooker he picked up in Brockton, Massachusetts and drove to a construction site. There, he raped her at knifepoint and then stabbed her to death. A short while later, Lewis was under arrest for attempted murder, after he tried to strangle a 5-year-old girl who lived in his apartment building. Ruled mentally unfit to stand trial, he was sent to Bridgewater State Hospital, where he would spend the next four years. When he was eventually brought to trial in 1992, Lewis entered a guilty plea, earning a 10-year sentence. With time served, he was out within six months, walking free in September 1992. Just two months later, he picked up a prostitute in Atlanta, Georgia, drove her out to a dirt road near Fulton County Airport, and there raped her at knifepoint before stabbing her to death.

Over the next few months, he would murder three more women, one of them heavily pregnant.

Lewis was accelerating, the time between kills getting shorter and shorter. But then, in October 1993, his murderous career came to a temporary halt when he started dating a woman named Kim Davis. For a time, all went well. Lewis stopped trolling for hookers and started looking for a job. But then, in December 1993, he followed Kim to a club and found her with another man. A fight ensued during which Lewis savagely beat both Davis and her new beau. He then fled the scene, sparking a high speed, 12-mile car chase before police officers ran him to ground. That escapade earned him a 10-year stretch, but he was out by November 1997, having served less than four years.

Lewis moved next to Daphne, Alabama where he found work at an auto repair shop. But he was soon cruising the streets again, looking for potential victims. On January 31, 1998, he raped, strangled and severely mutilated a 22-year-old hooker named Misty McGugin, later dumping her body in dense brush near U.S. 90. Just over two months later, on the evening of April 11, 1998, he picked up Kathleen Bracken at a local pool hall and took her a nearby motel.

Bracken met the same fate as Lewis's other victims. She was strangled into unconsciousness, raped, and then stabbed to death and mutilated. Lewis then took a shower before departing, leaving the bloody corpse behind.

But Lewis had been careless this time. Several witnesses had seen him talking to Kathleen Bracken at the pool hall, and he was soon under arrest. He almost immediately admitted to the murder, adding casually that he'd also killed Misty McGugin and five other women.

Gerald Patrick Lewis was convicted for the Bracken and McGugin murders and sentenced to death. He died in prison on July 25, 2009, of undisclosed causes. He remains a suspect in several other murders in Georgia, Alabama, and Massachusetts.

Louise Lindloff

In the city of Milwaukee, in the early 1900s, Louise Lindloff hawked her services as a clairvoyant. A woman with a flair for the dramatic, Lindloff would hold regular séances during which she'd gaze intently into her crystal ball and then lapse into an apparent trance. During that fugue state, she would convey messages from the spirit world to those in attendance, often speaking in a manly voice. Those who attended these sessions swore by the accuracy of her predictions, and it is true that her foretelling was sometimes remarkably precise. For example, she predicted that her 15-year-old son, Arthur Graunke Lindloff, would die on June 13, 1912, and the boy breathed his last on that very day. What the spirits didn't tell her was that she'd end up arrested and charged with his murder.

Lindloff was initially outraged by her arrest, but as she sat stewing in her cell, a calmness seemed to come over her. She told her jailors that she had consulted with her dead relatives in the afterlife and that they had assured her that the "cruel charges" against her would soon be withdrawn. This, unfortunately, was another piece of misinformation. Arthur's body had by now been autopsied and found to contain copious amounts of arsenic. Then a search was carried out at Mrs. Lindloff's home and turned up an arsenic-based rat poison, a box of mercurial poison, and several other bottles bearing a skull-and-crossbones insignia over the word "Toxic." This despite the fact that Lindloff had insisted to investigators that she kept no poisons on the property.

And by now the murder of Arthur Lindloff was not the only one being laid at the fortuneteller's door. Stories had begun to circulate about the untimely deaths of several other individuals connected to Lindloff, deaths from which she had profited handsomely, to the tune of over $10,000 in insurance money.

The first of those had occurred in August 12, 1905, when Mrs. Lindloff's first husband, Julius Graunke, died after a short illness, leaving his wife $2,000 richer. His death was attributed to sunstroke. Just two weeks later, Charles Lipschow, a boarder in the Lindloff household and reportedly Louise's lover, died of symptoms very similar to Julius Graunke. He left behind a $550 bequest to the widow.

In November 1906, the widow Graunke remarried, tying the knot with William LindloffMarital bliss in this case would last just under four years, with William passing from this world on August 3, 1910, apparently of heart disease. The intervening years, too, had been tainted by tragedy, marked by the deaths of Mrs. Lindloff's brother-in-law and her 22-year-old daughter, Frieda. In each of these cases, Lindloff cashed in an insurance policy. She'd cash another in August 1911, when her daughter Alma died suddenly at the age of 19. Alma had been in perfect heath until she was struck down by the mysterious ailment that took her life. The attending physician recorded cause of death as cardiac failure, after Louise assured him that Alma had always had a weak heart. Then, less than a year later came the sudden death of Arthur, the one that would lead to Mrs. Lindloff's arrest.

Yet, even with the autopsy report confirming lethal doses of arsenic in Arthur's system, Louise Lindloff remained adamant that she was innocent. She maintained that stance even when her deceased husbands and children were exhumed and found also to have been poisoned. Then another piece of evidence appeared. Apparently, Lindloff had predicted the deaths of each of her family members to her devotees. And her predictions had always been unfailingly accurate.

Louise Lindloff would nonetheless stand trial for only one murder, that of her son Arthur. Found guilty of that charge, she was sentenced to 25 years in prison. Most believed that she was lucky to avoid the gallows, but Lindloff was not long for this world in any case. She died in prison on March 9, 1914, apparently of cancer. Whether or not she predicted her own death is not recorded.

Will Lockett

At around 7:45 am on Wednesday, February 4, 1920, a farmer named Speed Collins was walking on his land in Fayette County, Kansas, when he came across a school satchel. Thinking that one of the students may have dropped it, he carried it to the nearby schoolhouse where teacher, Anna Young, identified it as belonging to 10-year-old Geneva Hardman. Geneva hadn't arrived for class that day, so the teacher sent two older boys to her house to ensure that she was all right. There, Geneva's mother told them that Geneva had left for school at 7:30, as usual. The anxious woman then joined the students in a search for the missing girl.

That search would soon be joined by several men from the area, and they almost immediately picked up the footprints of a large man and a child tracking together through the mud. Following those tracks brought them to a tragic scene. Geneva's body was found partly concealed by cattle fodder which had been pulled down over it. A large bloodstained rock lay nearby, and blood had also oozed from a horrific head wound and seeped into the child's clothing. One of the men ran immediately to fetch the Sheriff.

Now a second hunt was launched, this one involving several deputies equipped with bloodhounds. The hounds soon picked up a scent, leading the searchers towards Brannon Crossing. Along that route, they encountered a number of witnesses who reported seeing a local man named Will Lockett heading north "in a hurry." Locket was well-known to local law enforcement. He was a black military veteran who these days made his living by bootlegging and through petty theft and housebreaking. The police knew also that there were now several mobs out looking for him and that they were likely to lynch him if they found him first.

Fortunately for Lockett, it was the Sheriff's posse that ran him to ground, taking him into custody near Dixontown just after 4:30 pm that afternoon. From there, he was taken to Lexington and turned him over to the Lexington City Police. A dirty and blood-spattered pair of overalls that he'd been carrying at the time of his arrest was confiscated as evidence.

Shortly after his arrival at the police station, Lockett was questioned by Assistant Police Chief Ernest Thompson. During that interview, he confessed to killing Geneva Hardman, saying that he had snatched her as she crossed the field, carried her to a barn, and there tried to rape her. He hadn't succeeded because Geneva had put up such a fight. He'd then struck her on the head with a rock, killing her. Asked why he'd committed the murder, he replied simply, "I don't know."

From the moment that he confessed to the crime, Will Lockett was doomed. For a black man murdering a white child in the 1920s there could be only one outcome. Lockett was going to swing. But the good citizens of Lexington appeared unwilling to allow justice to take its course. Already there were rumors that a mob was gathering. Fearing a lynching, Assistant Chief Thompson ordered Lockett taken to the County Jail. From there, he was moved to the State Reformatory at Frankfort. When even that sturdy building was deemed vulnerable, he was moved to Louisville for his own safety.

The fact that Lockett didn't end up in the hands of a lynch mob can be put down to the foresight of the lawmen involved. At each of the locations where the prisoner had been held, huge mobs started gathering, sometimes missing his departure by mere minutes. The mobs only dispersed once their representatives were allowed to search the premises to confirm that Lockett wasn't there.

There was no hiding, though, when Lockett arrived in Lexington for his trial. By then news of the horrific murder had spread throughout the nation and troublemakers from across the state had streamed into town, intent on a lynching. Had the governor not called out the Kentucky National Guard, they might well have succeeded.

Inside the courtroom, meanwhile, the trial followed its predictable course. Since Lockett had pleaded guilty, no witnesses were called, and the entire business was concluded within 35 minutes. During that interlude, gunshots were heard frequently from outside as the mob tried to force its way into the building. Six civilians were killed in skirmishes and twenty wounded. Two soldiers were also injured in the fracas, but the line held long enough for the jury to find Lockett guilty and sentence him to death. The esteemed members of the jury had not even bothered to leave their seats before reaching their decision.

William Lockett was put to death in the electric chair at Eddyville State Prison on March 11, 1920. Three days before that execution, he asked to speak the warden, insisting that he wanted to "come clean." Before several witnesses, he confessed that he'd raped and killed three women, one black, and two white. One of these was later identified as Sally Kraft, whose decomposed remains had been found in Camp Taylor, a Louisville neighborhood. The other two victims remain unidentified.

Richard Macek

He was known as the "Mad Biter," a terrifying sobriquet, but one that is fully deserved in this case. Richard Macek, you see, got his kicks by ripping at his victims' flesh with his teeth. He also had one other bizarre fetish – he enjoyed mutilating his victims' eyelids after they were dead.

Born in McHenry, Illinois in 1948, Richard Otto Macek showed signs of his twisted psychology at an early age. He had just started junior high when he was arrested for stealing women's panties from clotheslines in his neighborhood. These were later found stashed in his room with the crotches apparently chewed away.

Macek walked away from that offense with no more than a stern warning. And he had apparently learned no lesson from it, because he was arrested again just months later, this time for peeking into windows. Macek wasn't your average Peeping Tom, though. Where perverts of that ilk normally try to catch a glimpse of naked flesh, Macek's preference was to watch women as they slept. Again, the punishment was a warning, and perhaps that encouraged him to go on to more serious offenses. In his late teens, he'd be the prime suspect in a series of attacks on women, although none of the victims could identify their attacker and so Macek was never charged.

Macek's next encounter with the law came after his girlfriend's baby died in his care. The infant expired after being left too long on a heating pad, but Macek claimed that it was negligence rather than murder and the authorities chose to believe him. Again, there was no punishment.

Fast forward to 1974 and Richard Macek was 26 years old, married and the father of two children. He was a short and stocky man with pudgy features, wispy blond hair and a face that somewhat resembled the Pillsbury Doughboy. But behind that seemingly benign exterior, a monster lurked, and on August 15, 1974 it emerged. Macek was staying at a hotel in Fontana, Wisconsin, when he cornered a 24-year-old maid named Paula Cupit in one of the rooms she was assigned to clean. The young woman was beaten into submission, then stabbed through the heart before Macek cut slits into her eyelids. He then attacked her dead body with her teeth, literally gnawing at her flesh the way a predator chews on a carcass. By the time the brutalized corpse was found later that afternoon, Macek was long gone.

Two months later, in Wauwatosa, Wisconsin, Macek struck again, throttling another hotel maid unconscious, then raping her and inflicting terrible wounds on her body. He then fled the scene believing his victim to be dead. Miraculously, she wasn't, and she was able to give the police a description of her assailant.

Unfortunately, that description got the police no closer to apprehending the "Mad Biter."

He showed up next in Crystal Lake, Illinois, where he inflicted his unique brand of mayhem on 26-year-old Nancy Lossman and her three-year-old daughter, Lisa, leaving behind a scene that several law officers described as the most gruesome they'd ever attended.

In July 1975, Macek attacked, raped and severely battered a 20-year-old woman at a Woodstock, Illinois laundromat. Then, with his identikit now decorating every police station and post office in the area, he fled west, taking up residence in San Bernardino, California. He was arrested there soon after and extradited to Wisconsin to face charges for the Wauwatosa rape.

While in custody, Macek was asked if he knew anything about the murder of Paula Cupit and he offered a unique response. He said that he didn't remember. A hypnotist was then brought in and, under hypnosis, Macek provided a description of the crime which exactly matched the evidence. That resulted in him being committed to Wisconsin's Central State Hospital for evaluation. Six months later, he was brought to trial in Illinois for the double homicide in Crystal Lake and the attempted murder in Woodstock. Found guilty, he drew a total term of 400 years. To that would later be added an additional life term in Wisconsin. The 'Mad Biter' also admitted to two additional murders, although he was never charged in those cases.

And neither would he serve out his well-deserved jail time. On March 2, 1987, Richard Macek was found hanging by a pair of bootlaces from an air vent in his cell. His death was ruled a suicide.

Joe Roy Metheny

Joe Roy Metheny was a serial killer and (if you believe his version of events) a cannibal, who sold his victims' flesh as pork to unsuspecting customers. Metheny's deadly rampage began in the summer of 1994 when he was working as a truck driver and living in South Baltimore, Maryland. He was married at the time, with a six-year-old son. But returning home from work one night, he found that his wife had cleared out the house and left with his boy. He would spend the next six months hunting for them all over Baltimore before he eventually tracked them to a crack house. There he learned that his wife and her current beau had been ejected from the house and were now living with a group of vagrants under a bridge on the other side of the city. He also found out that his wife had been arrested for prostitution a few months earlier and that his son had been taken away from her and made a ward of the state.

Infuriated by this, Metheny set out to get revenge. Driving to the bridge, he parked his car and got out carrying an ax. But his wife and her lover weren't there. Instead there were two homeless men passed out on a filthy mattress, and Metheny took out his frustrations on them, hacking them to death where they lay. Returning to the spot later, he found a doped-up prostitute and lured her under the bridge to see if she knew anything about his wife's whereabouts. She didn't and ended up hacked to death like the others.

Metheny would make several more visits to the bridge over the coming weeks. On each of those occasions, his wife and her lover were absent and he took out his anger on whoever he found there, killing three men and four women. He also murdered a couple of anglers who he thought might have seen him killing the homeless men. Their bodies (according to Metheny) were weighted down and sunk to the bottom of the stream. Years later, after he confessed, police divers would go searching for those bodies and find nothing.

And that perhaps might lead us to believe that Metheny was lying, talking himself up with his tales of wholesale slaughter. This is, of course, fairly common behavior among criminals, and perhaps it is true of Metheny. Perhaps he never killed a homeless person or a fisherman in his life. There can be little doubt, however, about the next four murders he committed.

By 1995, Metheny had given up his life on the road and was working for the Joseph Stein and Son pallet company and living in a trailer on the company's premises. On December 19, 1996, he met 26-year-old Kimberly Spicer at the Borderline Bar in Arbutus, Maryland. Spicer was lured back to his trailer where she was raped, stabbed and strangled before being buried less than 10 feet away from his front step, soon to be joined there by a second victim, Cathy Ann Magaziner. According to Metheny's later confession, he butchered both of the woman, barbequed their flesh, and sold them as beef and pork at an open-pit beef stand he was operating on the side. "The human body tastes very similar to pork," he told investigators. "If you mix it together, no one can tell the difference."

Metheny's claims of cannibalism have never been validated. However, he was definitely linked to a third murder, that of 28-year-old Toni Ingrassia, whose body had been found found in 1994 near Interstate 95, a short distance from the company where Metheny worked. Like the other victims, she had been stabbed and strangled. There was also a fourth victim, whose headless corpse was found buried in woodland close to the pallet factory.

Metheny had now murdered at least four women. And he might have continued indefinitely had he not made a mistake in December 1996, and allowed an intended victim to escape. Like the other women, Rita Kemper had been lured back to his trailer with the promise of cash for sex. She was barely through the door when Metheny grabbed her by the throat and started throttling her. Then, for some reason, he loosened his grip and Rita managed to wriggle free. Bolting from the trailer, she easily outpaced the obese Metheny, then scaled the fence and ran for her life. Later, when the police arrived, they found Joe meekly waiting for them. He surrendered without a fight.

Metheny confessed to ten murders but was charged with only three, since there was no evidence to support the other cases. At his trial, he begged the jury to sentence him to death and they were happy to oblige. The sentence was later commuted to life in prison, much to Metheny's disgust.

Joe Roy Metheny has continued to court controversy from behind bars with new revelations about his disgusting crimes. He now claims that after burying his victims, he dug them up to have sex with the rotting remains. As with his claims of cannibalism, we will never know the whole truth.

Donald Gene Miller

On New Year's Day of 1977, East Lansing, Michigan police officer Kenneth Ouellette received a call from a man named Gene Miller. Miller said that he was calling on behalf of Sue Young, whose daughter Martha had gone missing. The officer immediately sat up and took notice. He knew Martha Young, and he also knew her boyfriend, Donald, who was Gene Miller's son.

According to Miller Sr., Martha and Donald had been out on a date the previous evening after which he'd dropped her off at her parents' house. The young woman had not been seen or heard from since. After hanging up the phone, Officer Ouellette drove out to the Young residence where he found Sue Young and Gene Miller waiting for him. Also in attendance was a concerned looking Donald Miller who related how he'd dropped Martha off and then driven away without waiting to see that she'd gotten safely indoors.

But something about that explanation bothered Ouellette. Don Miller was a Criminal Justice graduate from Michigan State University. He and Martha were also churchgoers with conservative religious views. They were known to be close. The idea of Miller driving away, leaving his girlfriend standing all alone on a darkened street, just did not sit right with the officer. Pressed about it, Miller simply shrugged and said that he didn't think it would be a problem since he'd dropped Martha off right outside her house.

Over the days that followed, a search was launched for Martha Young. That search would ultimately fail, leaving investigators to turn their attention to the last person who had seen Martha alive, her boyfriend Donald Miller. Miller, though, was sticking steadfastly to his story. It would take the police months of investigative work before cracks began to appear in that story. During that time, Miller took two polygraph tests, failing both. And his complete lack of emotion when talking about his missing girlfriend was another red flag to investigators. They were sure that Miller was their man. The problem was that they did not have a shred of evidence to prove it.

Then, in October 1977, there was a break in the case. Martha Young's clothes were found in a field in Bath Township, neatly laid out on the ground as though she'd just floated out of them. The items were carefully bagged and sent to the state lab. But this was an era before DNA technology, and processing for fibers and other evidence came up empty. Donald Miller remained at large. And his continued freedom was about to have tragic consequences.

In June 1978, 28-year-old Marita Choquette vanished from her apartment in Grand Ledge, Michigan. Her body would be found two weeks later in the nearby town of Holt, on the same day that another young woman went missing. She was 21-year-old student Wendy Bush, last seen alive outside Case Hall on the MSU campus where Donald Miller worked as a security guard. Then, in August, another woman disappeared. Kristine Stuart was a 30-year-old middle school teacher who was living just blocks away from Don Miller's parental home on the day she mysteriously vanished.

East Lansing is a quiet town with a low crime rate and virtually no violent crime. And so the disappearances of four young women from its streets sent citizens into a panic and the local media into a near-frenzy. The police, meanwhile, stepped up patrols and urged residents to be vigilant. Just three days later, on August 15, those measures paid dividends. That was the day that Donald Miller entered a house in Delta Township and attacked a teenaged brother and sister. The girl, however, screamed so loudly that Miller eventually ran from the house, jumped into his car and sped away. As he did so, a neighbor jotted down his plate number, and by the end of the day, Miller was in custody.

The killer who had been plaguing East Lansing was finally off the street. But Miller was no fool. As a criminal justice graduate, he knew that the police had nothing on him besides an assault charge. It was only after the D.A. offered a deal, allowing him to plead to manslaughter, that he came clean and admitted to four murders. As part of that plea bargain, he later led officers to the bodies of Martha Young, Wendy Bush, and Kristine Stuart.

Miller would eventually plead guilty to two counts of manslaughter, two counts of assault and one count of criminal sexual conduct. He was sentenced to 50 years in prison with his earliest parole date in 1999. As that date approached, it inevitably sparked fear and outrage among East Lansing residents. Fortunately, Miller gave the authorities a reason to keep him behind bars when a garrote was found in his cell. An additional 20 years was added to his sentence. He next comes up for parole in 2018.

Stephen Morin

There can't be many death row inmates who refer to their execution as their "Graduation Day." But that was the case with Stephen Peter Morin. Morin, you see, had become a born-again Christian on Death Row and had decided that if the Lord wanted him to die, then he would submit to that authority. As a result, he waived all appeals and ended up strapped to a gurney at the Huntsville Unit in Texas on March 13, 1985, just four years after he'd been sentenced to death. But how had Morin ended up in this situation in the first place? To answer that question, we have to follow a lifelong journey of rape and murder during which the drug-addicted Morin became a suspect in thirty felonies and ended up on the FBI's most wanted list.

Stephen Morin was born on February 19, 1951 in Providence, Rhode Island. We don't know a lot about Morin's background, but we do know that he ended up in Nevada in the early '80s. There, he enjoyed taking long drives along the desolate stretches of highway that crisscross that state. And wherever Morin ventured, the bodies of dead and brutalized women seemed to turn up – 15-

year-old Kim Bryant, killed by blunt force trauma to the head; Linda Jenkins, beaten, strangled and then dumped in the desert; Susan Belotte, age 18, also strangled and dumped.

All of these the victims had been kidnapped from Las Vegas and murdered within the space of a single year between 1980 and 1981. But while the police strongly suspected that a single perpetrator was responsible, it was impossible to prove in those pre-DNA days. Stephen Morin, in any case, did not appear on any suspect list.

Then the discovery of a fourth victim, in an area appropriately named Hell Hole Canyon, finally put Morin in the frame. Like the other victims, Cheryl Ann Daniels had been abducted in Vegas and driven out to the desert. There, she had been raped, beaten and eventually strangled to death. But the killer had made a mistake this time. He'd dropped his wallet at the scene, and although it contained no identification, it did contain a note with the name and address of a young woman - Sara Pisan. Sara turned out to be a 19-year-old mother of three who was a co-worker of Cheryl Ann Daniels. Questioned by police, she said that the note had been written by a man named Andrew Generoso. Generoso, she said, had been pestering her to go out with him, but she had thus far spurned his advances because she found him "creepy."

The police now had a name and description of their suspect, even if the name they had was an alias. Andrew Generoso was actually Stephen Morin. And Morin had, in any case, quit the state. He'd always had a nose for trouble, and after realizing that he'd lost his wallet, he'd decided that it might be time to move on. Over the months that followed, he spent time in California and in Colorado before heading eventually to Texas.

In the early morning hours of December 11, 1981, 21-year-old Carrie Marie Scott was leaving her job at Maggie's Restaurant in San Antonio, Texas, when she found a man trying to hot-wire her car in the parking lot. Carrie yelled at the man but, to her surprise, he didn't run off. He continued fiddling under the dashboard, and in the next moment, the engine roared into life. The man then straightened up and warned Carrie to back off. She, however, was not about to allow her car to be taken without a fight. She angrily approached the car thief, but that was a bad mistake. Morin drew a gun and shot her dead where she stood.

But the shooting left Morin with a problem. He knew that the police would now be looking for the vehicle, and so he dumped it at a local shopping center. A short while later, he abducted another young woman, Margaret Palm, from that same center, forced her into her own car and told her to drive. But here, the story takes a decidedly strange twist. Rather than following his usual M.O. of driving his victim out into the wilderness to rape and kill her, Morin spent all day driving around with Palm in the car. Later, he instructed her to drop him off at a bus station in Kerrville, Texas and then told her that she was free to go. When the police arrived to arrest him a short while later, they found him reading a handwritten book of Bible verses which his captive had given him. He surrendered without a fight. Later, he'd credit Margaret Palm for converting him to Christianity by playing tapes of the Texas evangelist, Rev. Kenneth Copeland.

At the time of his arrest, Morin was suspected of at least thirty murders, with some law enforcement officials putting the number as high as 44. However, he was initially tried and convicted of just one –- Carrie Marie Scott. Later, on Death Row, he'd admit to murdering Janna Bruce in Corpus Christi, Texas and Shelia Whalen in Golden, Colorado. As for the other murders, Morin insisted that "Christ has wiped them from my memory."

Stephen Morin was executed by lethal injection on March 13th, 1985.

Stephen Nash

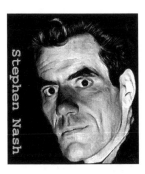

Friday was traditionally a bad day for finding laboring jobs. And so it was on the leaden November morning in 1956. The two men had waited for hours on a Skid Row corner without luck. Eventually, the younger of the two, 24-year-old Denis Butler suggested that they cut their losses and retire to a nearby bar. He had a few dollars and was buying. His companion, a tall wiry man with not a single tooth in his mouth, grunted his agreement.

Over beers, Butler learned a few things about his new friend, Stephen Nash. Nash had endured a difficult life. Abandoned as a baby, he'd had nothing but bad luck ever since, leaving him bitter with the world and humanity in general. He ranted on and on about his myriad grievances and how he'd like to take revenge for them. Some of his plans included multiple murder.

Butler probably took these outpourings of rage to be nothing but bluster because he invited Nash to join him for a meal. The two of them set off towards a Skid Row diner a few blocks away, with

Nash still raging and Butler letting him say his piece. Butler still did not take Nash's outburst seriously, but he had cause to regret that attitude when they reached the Third Street tunnel and his companion turned on him, holding a knife. Without a word, Nash attacked, driving the four-inch hunting blade into Butler's gut.

Butler screamed, then turned and ran, clutching the gaping wound to his stomach. He fled bleeding into the lobby of a nearby hotel, hoping the presence of other people would scare off his attacker. It did not. Nash followed and found Butler sprawled on the floor. He resumed his attack, pummeling the helpless man with his work boots, breaking his collar bone. Then he fled, leaving his victim unconscious on the ground.

Miraculously, Butler survived the attack and was able to give the police Nash's name and description. The attacker wasn't unknown to police. He'd spent several terms at San Quentin on charges of robbery and assault. A manhunt was immediately launched for Nash, who was considered a danger to the community at large. Sadly, they would not find him before he committed further atrocities.

Ten days after the attack on Denis Butler, Nash turned up in Long Beach, where he met John William Berg, a 27-year-old hairdresser. Berg made the grave mistake of inviting Nash back to his apartment and ended up stabbed to death. Three days later, on November 21, Nash lured ten-year-old Larry Rice to a spot under the Santa Monica Pier. Larry was later found lying in a pool of blood, over thirty stab wounds inflicted on his small frame.

As detectives began making inquiries into Larry Rice's murder, a clue emerged. A group of boys had seen Larry in the company of a tall, gaunt, toothless man. The description had a familiar ring to it. The police immediately began rounding up vagrants in Santa Monica and netted Nash just a day later.

Once in custody, Nash boastfully admitted to killing Larry Rice, saying he'd never killed a kid before and wanted to see what it felt like. He also confessed to killing the Long Beach hairdresser and trying to kill Denis Butler. But there was more. Nash launched into one of his trademark tirades, alternately boasting, crying and screaming. In between all that, he confessed to eight more murders, all committed within a six-week period between mid-October and late November.

Among Nash's victims were Floyd Leroy Barnett, a 27-year-old cannery worker, whose body had been found floating in the Sacramento River; merchant seaman William Clarence Burns, who Nash had beaten to death with a lead pipe; and Robert Eche, a 23-year-old draftsman for the Pacific Gas & Electric Company. Asked why he'd killed his victims, Nash explained that it was because they were better off than him. He then offered further confessions but said that the police would have to pay $200 for each additional murder. That offer was politely declined. There was already enough to send Nash to the gas chamber several times over.

Stephen Nash was tried and found guilty of murder and sentenced to death. He went to the gas chamber at San Quentin on August 21,

1959. Unrepentant until the last, Nash declared to the assembled press: "I'm the king of killers! I'll go to my death like a king should. I have nothing to die for because I had nothing to live for."

Joseph Naso

Joseph Naso was born in Rochester, New York, in 1934. Little is known about his early life, although we do know that he served in the Air Force in the 1950s, that he married a woman named Judith while in the service, and that he fathered a son named Charles who would later be diagnosed with schizophrenia. Perhaps due to the stresses of dealing with a mentally ill child, the marriage eventually broke down after 18 years, although Joe and Judith remained on good terms. After the divorce, Naso moved west, setting up home in San Francisco. Over the years that followed, he'd live in Oakland, Yuba City and Sacramento, as well as in Reno, Nevada. These addresses are important because in each of the cities that Joseph Naso called home, young women started turning up dead.

The first of those dead women was discovered on January 10, 1977. Roxene Roggasch was a petite and pretty 18-year-old who had only recently taken to prostitution. That career turned out to be a short one. Roxene was found dumped beside a road near Fairfax, California, a pair of pantyhose tightly knotted around her neck. No clues were found at the scene and, with no viable suspects, the case quickly went cold.

A year on and thirty miles away, another young prostitute was found dead by the roadside, in a crime that was remarkably similar to the Roggasch murder. Carmen Colon was 22 years old and she'd been strangled with a pair of pantyhose. Was this the work of the same killer? The police apparently didn't think so. Or maybe they just missed the connection. Prostitutes, after all, are convenient victims for all manner of psychos.

Fifteen years passed. Then in 1993, a third woman was found strangled and dumped in a rural area, this time in Yuba County, California. Unlike the earlier victims, Pamela Parsons was not a prostitute. The 38-year-old waitress did, however, have substance abuse problems. And she shared at least one unique characteristic with Roxene Roggasch and Carmen Colon, her matching initials. RR, CC, PP; was that a clue or just coincidence? The police had no way of knowing. They were still in the dark a year later when another strangled corpse was found in Yuba County, this time dumped in a cemetery. She was 31-year-old Tracy Tafoya and she'd been drugged, raped and strangled.

The mystery of the matching initial victims remained unresolved over the next decade and a half. Then on April 13, 2010, the case took a sharp turn towards resolution when a parole officer named Wes Jackson paid a surprise visit to Joe Naso's home in Reno, Nevada.

Naso was, at the time, serving a period of probation, after being arrested for shoplifting. And Jackson soon discovered a violation of his release conditions, a bullet lying in an ashtray on the coffee table. This prompted the parole officer to call in the police to carry out a more thorough search of the house. It was during that search that they found Naso's macabre photograph collection, including several in which the subject was posed in a position meant to imitate death. Judging by the marbling of the skin in some of the pictures, not all of the shots were simulated. Marbling is a telltale sign of decomposition.

Even more incriminating was Naso's diary, in which he had recorded details of multiple attacks on women, including a page headed 'List of Ten.' Investigators theorized that these were references to murders Naso had committed, and further inquiries only strengthened that belief. The cryptic clues alluded to, among others, the murders of Roxene Roggasch, Carmen Colon and Tracy Tafoya. There was also a reference to Pamela Parsons, described by Naso as, "a girl from Yuba County." Pamela's photograph was among the "corpse shots" found in Naso's collection. Later, investigators would submit the pantyhose used to strangle Roggasch for DNA analysis. It delivered two DNA profiles. One was matched to Naso's ex-wife Judith. The other was matched to Naso himself.

Joseph "Crazy Joe" Naso appeared for trial at the courthouse in Marin County, California on April 13, 2011. He stood accused of four murders – Roxene Roggasch, Carmen Colon, Pamela Parsons and Tracy Tafoya. He insisted on conducting his own defense, but his incoherent babbling and frequent tirades did him few favors. Found guilty of four counts of first degree murder, Naso was sentenced to death. He currently awaits execution at San Quentin State Prison. Given his age, it is unlikely that the sentence of the court will ever be carried out. Naso will, however, die in prison.

But many questions about the case still remain unanswered, most pressing among those the issue of the New York Alphabet Murders? DNA evidence in the case suggests that Naso is not responsible for those murders, although they may well have inspired him to go on his own killing spree. We will never know for certain.

Darren O'Neall

Darren Dee O'Neall was born in Albuquerque, New Mexico, on February 26, 1960. We don't know much about his childhood, but we do know that he grew to be a drifter, fashioning himself on the heroes from books by his favorite author, Louis L'Amour. We know also that he was a bit of a lady's man, reasonably good-looking and with a glib line of talk that made him successful with the opposite sex. Darren, though, wasn't much interested in sweet-talking women. He preferred to take his conquests by force.

On the evening of March 28, 1987, 22-year-old Robin Smith was drinking at a tavern in Puyallup, Washington, when she struck up a conversation with a man who introduced himself as Herb Johnson. Robin was due to attend a house party that night, and so she asked the host to invite her new acquaintance. O'Neall drove there in his own car, following Robin and her fiance Larron Crowston. But Crowston had to leave early, and so Johnson offered to drive Robin home. She was never seen alive again, although detectives did find her bloodstained jacket and several of her teeth inside the trunk of Herb Johnson's abandoned car.

The car, as it turned out, did not belong to Johnson at all. It had been stolen two months earlier from a truck driver in Nampa, Idaho. The trucker remembered the thief well. He said that he'd picked him up hitchhiking and had offered him a place to sleep for the night. When he woke the next morning, the man was gone and so, too, was his car, a Chrysler New Yorker. The man had also stolen his Ruger .357 revolver, he said. He described the man as twenties, around 6- oot tall and slim, with blond hair. The word "JUNE" was tattooed across the knuckles of his left hand.

That last piece of information was particularly helpful. As detectives began scanning through records, they came across a man named Darren O'Neall who had just such a tattoo and also matched the general description. O'Neall was currently wanted for skipping out on child support payments.

On April 29, 1987, Wendy Aughe, 29, disappeared after leaving her beauty school night class. Wendy's friends told police that she'd had a date that night with a bartender working at restaurant in Bellingham, Washington. When detectives went to question the man, they found that he had walked out on his job, not even returning to collect his paycheck. Fingerprints lifted from his employment application identified him as Darren O'Neall. When Wendy's car turned up a few days later outside a tavern in Eugene, Oregon, federal warrants were issued charging O'Neall with unlawful flight to avoid prosecution for murder.

By that time, there were two more murders linked to the elusive O'Neall. Lisa Szubert had disappeared from a truck stop at Mountain Home, Idaho, where she'd last been seen talking to a tall man bearing the now familiar knuckle tattoo. She was found dead on June 13, southeast of La Grande, Oregon. And Robin Smith had been found, her skeletal remains turning up near Greenwater, Washington, in the shadow of Mt. Rainier. In addition, there was a sexual assault in Colorado Springs, where the victim identified O'Neall as her assailant. Another woman barely escaped being abducted by O'Neall in Burly, Idaho, while in Salt Lake City, three women were shot to death. Each had been seen in the company of a man with the word JUNE tattooed across his knuckles. With the body count mounting, O'Neall was added to the FBI's "Most Wanted" list on June 25.

Darren O'Neall was finally arrested in Lakeland, Florida on February 3, 1988, after he was pulled over in a routine traffic stop and found to be driving a stolen vehicle. In January 1989, he was extradited to Washington to stand trial for the murder of Robin Smith. However, during jury selection, he abruptly announced that he wanted to plead guilty. As a result, he received a life sentence, which in Washington means a maximum term of 27 years and 9 months. He could technically be out in 18 years with time off for good behavior.

However, O'Neall still had other crimes to answer for. In May 1990, he was brought to Portland, Oregon, to face trial for the kidnapping and rape of a 14-year-old girl. O'Neall protested his innocence, but to no avail. He was found guilty of all charges and sentenced to 135 years in prison.

O'Neall has never been charged with the murders of Wendy Aughe and Lisa Szubert. However, given the time he has to serve in

Washington and Oregon, it is unlikely that he will ever be a free man.

William Pierce

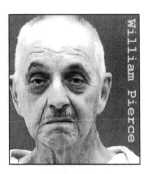

Ironically, it is for a murder that he probably didn't commit that William Pierce achieved his 15 minutes of fame. Twelve-year-old Peg Cuttino had set off to walk the few blocks to her sister's elementary school in Sumter, South Carolina on the morning of December 18, 1970. Somewhere along that route, Peg disappeared. Twelve days later, on December 30, two airmen from the nearby Shaw Air Force Base were riding trail bikes in Manchester State Forest when they came upon a figure lying on the ground, partially covered by vegetation. At first, they thought that it was a mannequin, but then they spotted the polka-dot sash, such as the one Peg had reportedly been wearing at the time of her disappearance. The men pedaled quickly to a nearby general store and called the police. A pathologist would later determine that the little girl had been raped and sodomized before being bludgeoned to death, most probably with a tire iron.

The rape and murder of such a young child caused outrage in Sumter. And the police were placed under extra pressure to catch the killer because of who Peg Cuttino was. Her father was State Senator James Cuttino. Did that affect Sheriff Byrd Parnell's handling of the investigation? Perhaps. Suffice to say that police attention quickly zoned in on a habitual criminal named William "Junior" Pierce and that Junior, just as quickly, confessed.

Junior wasn't the sharpest tool in the box. In fact, with an IQ that "barely broke 70," he was borderline retarded. Still, he loved to play games with the cops, believing always that he had the upper hand on them. The fact that he was sitting in a Georgia jail cell, facing charges for nine different murders when Sheriff Parnell arrived to question him, says different.

Pierce would never have even appeared on the radar in the Cuttino murder had he not hinted to Sheriff Red Carter of Appling County, Georgia, that he had something to say on the matter. That had prompted Carter to make a call to his counterpart in Sumter and had brought Parnell south at his earliest opportunity.

According to Junior's statement, he had rescued Peg Cuttino from an altercation with a teenaged boy at a drive-in restaurant in Sumter. Then, after the boy had driven off, Peg had got voluntarily into his car. He'd driven her to a landfill on the edge of town, but Peg had started crying and asking him to take her home. He'd then (for no reason he could adequately explain) taken a tire iron and hit her over the head.

It was a quite ridiculous story and one that any investigator worth his salt would have dismissed out of hand. Parnell, however, seems to have ignored everything that conflicted with the evidence and bought what Pierce had to say. Later, Pierce would disavow his statement and say that he'd been threatened with torture if he refused to confess. Nonetheless, the matter made it all the way to trial and Junior Pierce was ultimately found guilty and sentenced to life in prison.

There are those who insist, to this day, that Pierce was railroaded for the Cuttino murder. But that in no way means that he was an innocent man. There were the nine murders that had landed him in the Georgia jail in the first place. Those, with varying degrees of certainty, can be laid squarely at Pierce's door. Among them were the murders of Kathy Anderson, a 17-year-old waitress from Columbia, South Carolina; Ann Goodwin, an 18-year-old Winthrop University student; and Virginia Mains, a 20-year-old housekeeper from Gastonia, North Carolina. Evidence also connects Pierce to the murders of James L. Sires, Lacy Thigpen, Joe Fletcher, Vivian Miles and Hazel Wilcox, all of them owners or employees of small country stores or gas stations across Georgia and the Carolinas.

FOOTNOTE: In later years, Pee Wee Gaskins, one of America's most notorious serial killers, confessed that it was he who had murdered Peg Cuttino. Gaskins's confession sounds a lot more feasible than the one given by Pierce, and he was working on a building site in Sumter at the time Peg was killed. The 12-year-old would have walked directly past the site on the day she disappeared.

Gaskins was never charged with the Cuttino murder. He was executed in the electric chair in 1991 for a series of unrelated crimes.

Mark Antonio Profit

The term "career criminal" was probably created with a man like Mark Profit in mind. A native of Minneapolis, Profit had been in and out of prison since the age of 15 on a range of offenses that virtually defined the Minnesota Criminal Code. Fast forward 18 years to 1996, and the 33-year-old Profit had lived only a single year outside of a correctional institution. He was free now, however, and determined to make the most of that freedom.

1996 was also the year that the City of Lakes experienced one of its most horrific murder sprees. Between May and July of that year, four prostitutes turned up dead in the vicinity of Theodore Wirth Park or inside the park itself.

It began on May 8 when the body of Renee Bell was found floating in Basset Creek, a stream that flows through the park. She'd died from ligature strangulation. Then, with the police no closer to solving that crime, another murder was uncovered, this one more gruesome than the first. Like Renee Bell, 43-year-old Deborah LaVoie had a record for prostitution; like Bell she'd ended up dead in the park. In this case, however, the killer had doused the corpse with gasoline and lit it on fire in an apparent effort to destroy forensic evidence.

Prostitute murders are, of course, an all too common tragedy. So at this point, the police were not jumping to any conclusions. At this point, the murders were officially regarded as separate incidents.

Within two weeks, however, Minneapolis PD would have cause to revisit that opinion. That was when another hooker turned up strangled to death. Avis Warfield, 36, was found on June 19, not inside the park but close enough to suggest a connection to the other dead women.

The story was, by now, receiving heavy circulation in the local media with headlines about the "Wirth Park Killer" dominating the front pages. And the authorities responded accordingly, beefing up patrols in and around the park. For a time, it worked, with the killer driven to ground by the increased police presence. But six weeks later, on July 29, there was another murder. Keooudorn Photisane, a 21-year-old male transvestite, was found strangled to death near a bike path on the Theodore Wirth golf course, adjacent to the park.

To the general public, it must have appeared that the police were making very little progress in the case. In fact, they already had a strong suspect in their sights. On July 13, an officer patrolling in the park had found a wallet lying on the bank of Basset Creek, just a few feet from where Renee Bell's body had been found. Among other things, the wallet contained the driver's license of Mark Antonio Profit.

Profit, of course, was well-known to law enforcement, with a rap sheet that included convictions for rape and assault. But the wallet alone was not sufficient cause to arrest him. It was only after a man named Paul Kelly, the brother of Profit's girlfriend, was questioned that the pieces began to slot together. Kelly told police that Profit had borrowed a gas canister from him on the night

Deborah LaVoie was murdered and her body set on fire. That same evening, he'd seen Profit washing stains out of the clothes he'd been wearing. The following day, Profit had asked for his help in cleaning his car and had spent a long time scrubbing the seats and carpet. Kelly also claimed to have seen a letter, written by Profit, in which he confessed to killing Keooudorn Phothisane.

On August 2, officers executed a search warrant at Profit's home and took custody of his 1990 Pontiac Grand Am. Fibers lifted from the car would prove to be chemically identical to those from the ligature with which Renee Bell had been strangled. Another woman had also come forward to testify that Profit had lured her to Wirth Park with the offer of sharing some crack cocaine. Once there, he'd ordered her to perform oral sex on him. When she'd refused, he'd grabbed her by the throat and threatened to kill her. She might well had died that night, but a couple were driving through the park at that time and spotted the altercation. The couple, together, had run Profit off. Later, they'd pick him out of a photo array as the assailant.

Mark Profit was arrested on October 3, 1996, and charged with the murder of Renee Bell. Subsequent DNA evidence would link him with at least one of the other Wirth Park victims, but Profit would be convicted only of the Bell murder and of assaulting Phynnice Johnson, the woman who had escaped his clutches. Those crimes were enough to earn his two life terms.

In October 2001, Mark Profit was found dead in his cell at the Minnesota Correctional Facility in Oak Park Heights. His death was ruled a suicide.

Todd Alan Reed

By some definitions of the term, Todd Alan Reed would be called a spree killer rather than a serial killer, such was the ferocity of his onslaught against Portland, Oregon streetwalkers in 1999. Within the space of just four blood-soaked weeks, Reed brutally snuffed out the lives of three women, leaving their broken bodies discarded like trash in a densely wooded Portland park. He is also a suspect in several other murders, committed over a decade earlier.

To those who knew Todd Reed, though, the idea that he could have committed these murders would have seemed ludicrous. To them, he was a devoted father who held down two jobs to support his sons and wrote poetry in his spare time. And yet, Todd Reed was far from an innocent. His life, in fact, was a near blueprint for the making of a serial killer

Born in Portland, Oregon on May 22, 1967, Reed had endured a difficult childhood. His parents divorced when he was four, leaving him devastated since he'd had a close bond with his father. Later, when his mother remarried, Todd became increasingly withdrawn, although his relationship with his stepfather, Robert Reed, later thawed somewhat. Then, just when things appeared to be on an even kilter, Todd's mother and Robert Reed divorced. It was a short while later that Todd got into his first trouble with the law, picked up on a burglary charge. By 14, he was in a residential program for at-risk youths, remaining there until his eighteenth birthday.

In the summer of 1986, Reed, now 19, met a 15-year-old girl
named Gail Bennett. The two of them were soon cohabitating,
although the conditions were hardly ideal. Sometimes they
crashed with friends, and when their welcome wore thin, they'd
live in a tent in some field. They also had no money for food, and so
Reed returned to his old hobby of house-breaking. That led to an
arrest in 1987 from which Reed was lucky to escape without a
custodial service.

And perhaps that close shave taught him a lesson. In October
1988, he and Gail got married, ironically in front of the same judge
who had earlier tried Reed for burglary. Soon after, he started
working at a Sizzler restaurant and later worked at a fruit
distributor and then at a Safeway store.

But while Reed appeared to have turned his life around on the
outside, he was secretly living out his depraved fantasies through
porn magazines and phone sex-lines. Within a year, he'd crossed
the line from fantasy into reality, forcing a pregnant woman into
his car at knifepoint and making her perform oral sex on him. He
also made a half-hearted attempt to strangle her with a seat „belt
but soon let her go. The woman went straight to the police and
Reed was arrested. At trial, he entered a plea of no contest and was
sentenced to seven years. He walked free in 1995, having served
just three.

Gail had stuck by her husband while he served his time, but in
1997, she finally called time on the marriage. Reed was ordered to

pay child support for the couple's two sons and was granted visits with his sons every other weekend. With plenty of time now on his hands and no one to tell him otherwise, he began cruising regularly for prostitutes. Within two years, those nightly excursions would turn deadly.

Between May 7, 1999, and June 2, 1999, the corpses of three prostitutes – Lilla Faye Moler, 28; Stephanie Lynn Russell, 26; and Alexandria Nicole Ison, 17 – were found discarded in a remote part of Forest Park in Portland. Each of the women had been strangled, and detectives couldn't help noticing that they bore a striking resemblance to each other. Fearing that they might have a serial killer on their streets, Portland PD immediately set up the Forest Park Task Force. One of their first moves was to set a trap for the killer. A female police officer, who bore some resemblance to the victims, was sent undercover to pose as a prostitute on West Burnside Street, a popular pickup spot. It wasn't long before she'd netted a suspect. Todd Reed pulled up in his black Mitsubishi Eclipse and suggested that the undercover cop get in and go for a ride with him.

That, of course, was never going to happen. While Reed was still trying to entice the undercover cop into his car, a police car pulled up and an officer stepped out. Reed was asked to provide I.D. and he did so willingly, handing over his driver's license. He also told the sergeant, without being asked, that he was a convicted sex offender. When the officer asked if he could search the car, Reed agreed right away, although the search produced nothing of interest, other than a novel about a serial killer. Reed was then allowed to drive away.

His respite, however, would be only temporary. While the cops had been running their undercover operation, they had also been pursuing other leads. The most important of these was a used condom found near one of the crime scenes and a semen stain lifted from the thigh of one of the victims. Reed, of course, had a DNA profile on record, thanks to his 1992 conviction. Now the police had a match. Reed was arrested soon after.

At his trial, Todd Reed entered guilty pleas to all three murders, earning him a sentence of life in prison. He remains the chief suspect in the 1987 murders of Mindi Thomas, 12, and Jennifer Tchir, 15.

Monte Rissell

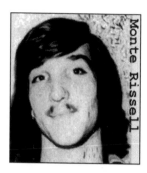

It was clear from a very early age that Monte Rissell was going to come to no good. Born in Alexandria, Virginia in 1959, Rissell was just 14 years old when he committed his first rape. He was sitting in a high school biology class when police officers arrived to arrest him.

Rissell was sent to a reformatory but, in truth, there was very little that the law could do to him, no matter how serious his crimes. And even the high walls and fences of his new home proved no deterrent to the juvenile rapist. He escaped often and, during those escapes, continued his sexual assaults on women. On one occasion, he even raped a woman in the parking lot of the school.

Yet even as Rissell was continuing his campaign of terror, he was sweet talking his counselors into believing that he was a changed man. To them, he appeared the perfect inmate, respectful and different and, on the surface at least, deeply sorry for the pain he'd caused. Such duplicitous behavior is, of course, typical of the psychopath, and there can be little doubt that Monty Rissell was one of those. Still, his repentance was taken as genuine and, in 1976, the now 18-year-old Rissell was back on the streets. Five young women would pay a dreadful price for his freedom.

Would Rissell have committed his dreadful crimes without a catalyst to tip him over the edge? That question is impossible to answer except to refer to other, similar cases and to suggest that Rissell would have graduated to murder, no matter what. As it was, there was a convenient excuse that he could later blame for his actions – a breakup with his girlfriend. Rissell had begun dating the girl shortly after his release but she'd soon tired of his possessiveness and had called time on the relationship, ending things in a letter. Determined to confront the girl, Rissell had gotten into his car and had driven to the college where she was a student. There, he'd spotted her walking hand-in-hand on campus with another man, leaving him fuming.

Rather than confront the girl and her new boyfriend, Rissell had driven away, stopped off at a liquor store to buy a quart of vodka, and then driven home. He'd sat in his car in the parking lot, pulling on the bottle and getting progressively drunk as the afternoon slid towards dusk. It was around seven p.m. that he saw a lone woman pull into the lot and felt his slow-burning anger stir again. He quelled it just long enough to call out to the woman and offer her a slug of vodka. To his surprise, she not only came over but slid into the passenger seat.

What Rissell hadn't known when he'd called out to her was that the woman was a prostitute. When he suggested sex, she willingly agreed, at a price. Rissell then suggested that they take a drive and find a spot, which the woman agreed to. Once there, they started having sex and Rissell's anger bubbled to the surface once more. He got his hands around the woman's throat and started throttling her. She, however, managed to knee him in the groin and break free. She jumped from the car and made a run for it, putting distance between herself and her attacker until she tripped on a stump and went tumbling into a ravine. As she lay injured at the bottom, Rissell slid down after her. He clubbed her over the head with a rock, then dragged her to a small stream and held her head underwater until she drowned.

Rissell was emboldened by his first murder, thrilled by it. He soon went hunting again, now carrying a hunting knife with a wickedly serrated edge. Over the next eight months, four more women would have the distinct misfortune of crossing paths with him. Each of them ended up raped and stabbed to death, the mutilations becoming more severe with each crime. His final victim, killed in 1977, would suffer nearly 100 cuts and stab wounds. Thankfully, he was arrested soon after. Just nineteen years old, he had already committed five horrific mutilation murders.

Monte Rissell was sentenced to five life terms for his crimes, although in this case, life did not actually mean life. Frighteningly, Rissell was released on parole in 2012.

Gary Robbins

On the evening of April 14, 1988, a man forced his way into a house in Brothersvalley, Pennsylvania and attacked Mary Ann Marker, wife of a state trooper. His intention was obviously to rape Mrs. Marker, but she put up fierce resistance, refusing to yield even when he drew a gun and threatened to shoot her. Frustrated, the man eventually made good on his threat, shooting Mrs. Marker in the face. He then ran from the house, jumped into his car and drove off.

But his timing could hardly have been any worse. At that very moment, a colleague of Mrs. Marker's husband was driving by the house. Seeing an unfamiliar man fleeing the premises, the trooper followed, radioing for backup at the same time. A high speed chase ensued, with other police vehicles joining in the pursuit along Route 219. Eventually, the fugitive was boxed in. After firing a few wild shots at the police, he put the gun in his mouth and ended his own life. While all of this was going on, Mary Ann Marker had been rushed to hospital where emergency surgery would save her life. She would later make a full recovery.

Identifying the dead man was an easy job for the police. He was driving a rental car which he'd hired using a credit card in the name of Gary A. Robbins. That turned out to be his own name rather than an alias. Inside the car, police found two guns, a roll of duct tape and a length of nylon rope. They believed this to be a "rape kit."

But that was just a foretaste of what was to come. Searching
Robbins's home, investigators uncovered a cache of items that
marked their man out as a sexual deviant – studded leather belts,
vibrators, handcuffs, a Polaroid camera, gags, and several books
with gruesome pictures of extreme sadomasochism. The police
were also aware by now that Robbins had a record. He'd served
time for armed robbery and for assaulting two women in Ohio in
1970. Those offenses would soon pale, though, compared to what
Robbins had been doing in the eighteen years since.

Robbins was a traveling salesman who hawked life insurance door
to door. That allowed him to travel extensively, and he apparently
used these business trips as a cover for his more nefarious
pursuits. Investigators were soon building a case against him for a
series of murders and sexual assaults committed across his area of
operation. There was strong evidence linking him to sex slayings
in Steubenville, Ohio; Reed City, Michigan; Bel Air, Maryland; and
Chester, West Virginia. In addition, Robbins was linked to the
murder of Carol Jursik, a talented fencer who was tipped to make
the US Olympic team. Evidence also tied him to sexual assaults on
women in Center Township, Pennsylvania and Timonium,
Maryland.

In order to understand Robbin's M.O., investigators revisited the
terrifying ordeal of a nurse from Butler County, Pennsylvania. This
woman was one of the few to escape the serial killer, and she had a
harrowing tale to tell. She said that she was approached by a man
who asked if he could view her house, which was on the market at
that time. Since he was well presented and articulate, she had
willingly allowed him into her home. But he was barely through
the door when he'd turned on her. She was bound and gagged,

then forced into the stranger's car and driven to an isolated spot in Greene County. There she was repeatedly raped while her assailant recorded it all, snapping away with a Polaroid camera. He then started torturing her, whipping her, singeing her hair and burning her with cigarettes. Then he throttled her into unconsciousness and (presumably believing that she was dead) threw her from the car. The woman woke up later, naked in a field and in extreme pain. Somehow she managed to make it to the road and flagged down a motorist who took her to the hospital. She later picked Gary Robbins's picture from a photo array as the man who had attacked her.

Most of the other victims told a similar story, of being attacked by a well-dressed, smooth-talking man who they had allowed to view their homes. And a search of car rental records showed that Robbins was in each of the areas at the time that these attacks occurred. We will never know for certain how many women he killed, but police estimate that it is at least five and probably more.

John Francis Roche

The city of New York has produced its fair share of monsters over the decades, from depraved cannibal Albert Fish, to psychotic shooter David Berkowitz, to nerdy prostitute ripper Joel Rifkin. One murderous New Yorker who is less well known, although just as evil, is a killer from the 1950s, a heartless ogre by the name of John Francis Roche.

Roche was born to poor Irish immigrants in 1927. Both of his parents were alcoholics and both died young, leaving the boy to make his own way on the tough streets of Brooklyn. That saw him in trouble with the law from an early age and packed off to reform school before he'd even reached puberty. There, he learned very little, other than how to be a better criminal.

Released in 1945, at the age of 18, Roche worked a number of low-paying jobs. He was a delivery boy for a time, then a factory worker and then a plumber's helper. But there were easier pickings to be had, and for much less effort. He soon reverted to his old habit of breaking and entering, landing him in jail within a year. Not that it discouraged him. Almost immediately after his release, he was back in the game. Only now, he carried an array of weapons – a butcher's knife, an icepick and a lead pipe. One prison stretch had been enough for Roche. Anyone who got in his way from now on would be silenced.

On November 15, 1953, Roche was burglarizing a property on East 66th Street in Yorkville when he was surprised the householder, 85-year-old Rosa Chronik. The elderly woman would have been capable of very little resistance, but Roche nonetheless employed his icepick to silence her, inflicting eleven deep wounds on his frail victim and leaving her bleeding to death on the floor.

That murder apparently left him with a taste for it. Five months after killing Mrs. Chronik, he claimed another victim, a 17-year-old waitress named Marion Brown. The young woman was found raped and stabbed to death in the hallway of her apartment building in April 1954. A month later, Roche knifed a cab driver to death and made off with the money he was carrying.

And then came the murder that would propel John Francis Roche from petty criminal to the most reviled man in New York City. On the morning of June 2, a woman named Mae Sullivan was descending the stairs at her apartment building on East 66th Street when she heard a distinct groan. In the next moment, a man emerged from the shadows, pushed past and walked quickly away, muttering the words, "She's sick," over his shoulder. Sullivan then followed the groans to under the staircase, where she found her 14-year-old neighbor, Dorothy Westwater, lying on the ground.

The girl was barely clinging on to life. She was rushed to the hospital where it was found that she had been

bludgeoned and stabbed. She had also been raped.

Three days later, NY Patrolman Gus Roniger pulled over a dark-colored Pontiac in Rockaway Beach, Queens. The car proved to be stolen, and the cop also spotted a bloody pipe and knife in the foot-well. The sharp-eyed officer also noticed that the driver bore a resemblance to the man wanted in connection with the Westwater attack and that there were flecks of dried blood on his clothing. He therefore took the man, John Roche, into custody.

Back at the precinct, detectives started their interrogation of Roche by asking him to account for his whereabouts over the last few days. They were not prepared for the response he gave. "On Wednesday I attacked that girl in the city," he said. He then went on to confess to the murders of Marion Brown, Rosa Chronik and cabbie Alexander Jablonka. Two days later, a fourth murder charge was added to his rap sheet when Dorothy Westwater died of her injuries.

One might wonder why Roche confessed so easily to the murders. Many commentators at the time speculated that he was trying to create the basis for an insanity defense, but the killer was quick to clear up that misapprehension. "I don't want to go to jail," he said in a press interview, "and I don't want to be sent to an insane asylum. I just want to die."

Given the crimes that Roche had committed and the era in which he had committed them, it was always likely that his death wish would be granted. Despite the valiant efforts of the defense attorney to have him declared insane, Roche was deemed responsible for his actions, guilty as charged and eligible for the death penalty. He met his end in the electric chair at Sing Sing Prison on January 26, 1956.

Gary Lee Schaefer

At around 4:30 p.m. on the pleasant spring afternoon of April 9, 1983, friends Caty Richards and Rachel Zeitz decided to get some pizza. The 11-year-olds had spent the afternoon hanging out at Caty's house in Springfield, Vermont until hunger pangs sent them in the direction of the local pizzeria. When they arrived however, the place was crowded, and the girls decided they didn't want to wait. That turned out to be a fateful decision. As the girls were on their way back, a car pulled up beside them and a man leaned across and asked for directions. Then he suddenly popped the door and got out of the vehicle. He told the girls that he had a gun and would kill them unless they did exactly what he said.

Faced with this threatening stranger, the girls responded in very different ways. Rachel turned and immediately sprinted away, crossing an empty lot and then scaling a small hillock. Caty froze and remained rooted to the spot. When Rachel looked back she saw her friend being forced into the man's car. Then, as the vehicle sped away, Rachel ran to the nearest house and asked the residents to call the police.

Police officers were soon on the scene, and to them Rachel was able to provide a description of the abductor. She was particularly adamant about a sweatshirt the man had been wearing and told police that a boy in her class had one exactly like it. The boy was then traced, and his father told police that the shirt had been made for an event at a local church. As far as he knew, only one adult member of the congregation had been given such a shirt, 31-year-old parishioner Gary Schaefer.

The police now had a suspect, but they erred in not launching an immediate search, instead sending officers to stake out Schaefer's home and the auto workshop where he worked. They also prevented Caty's parents from launching their own search for their missing child, insisting that they should "leave it to the professionals." Had they started looking immediately, it is possible that the little girl might have been found alive. As it was, her body was discovered at 2 p.m. the following day. She had been savagely raped and beaten so badly that she was only recognizable by her braces and the spray of freckles across the bridge of her nose. Autopsy results suggested that she'd died at around 8 p.m. the previous evening. Later that afternoon, her suspected killer was taken into custody when he returned to his residence.

Gary Lee Schaefer was a Vermont native born in 1951. He had lived an apparently normal life until he enlisted in the Navy in 1970. That was when a darker side to his personality emerged, and he was charged variously with arson and drugs offenses. At his court martial, Schaefer claimed insanity, but Navy psychiatrists found him competent to stand trial He was ultimately convicted and dishonorably discharged from the service. Thereafter, Schaefer returned to his native Springfield where he worked various jobs before settling on a career as an auto mechanic. He also began attending the strictly fundamentalist Christadelphian Church.

On the surface, it appeared that Schaefer had settled into a stable existence. Friends and family, in fact, found him overly meek, overly quiet. But there was another side to Schaefer, one that he kept hidden from the world. He was obsessed with pornography and consumed with a simmering lust for young girls. In 1979, that simmer came to a boil.

That was the year that Schaefer committed his first murder, raping and killing 13-year-old Sherry Nastasia. Sherry's family lived in an apartment building managed by Schaefer's brother, but there was nothing to suggest that Schaefer might be the killer. Neither were there any clues when 14-year-old Theresa Fenton suffered a near identical fate in 1981.

But less than a year later, the police did have a lead on Schaefer when a 16-year-old escaped his clutches in nearby Brattleboro. The girl later provided a description which matched Schaefer to a tee. Unfortunately, there was no corroborating evidence and Schaefer remained at large. His continued liberty would have tragic consequences for young Caty Richards.

Now there was considerable concern for other young girls in Springfield when the police were again forced to release Schaefer due to lack of evidence. He would remain free for nearly six months until a dramatic turn of events. Caty Richards's mother had written to Schaefer urging him to confess his sins, according to the tenets of his church. In September 1983, he did just that, admitting to the murders of Caty Richards and Theresa Fenton. He also confessed to the rape of Deana Buxton, the 16-year-old who had managed to get away from him.

In December 1983, Schaefer pled guilty to the kidnapping, sexual assault, and second-degree murder of Caty Richards. (All other charges were dropped as part of his plea agreement.) He was sentenced to 30 years to life, that time to be served at the federal penitentiary in Leavenworth, Kansas.

David Spanbauer

Born in Oshkosh, Wisconsin in 1941, David Spanbauer took to criminality at an early age, racking up a catalog of juvenile offenses. At 17, he dropped out of school and joined the Navy, a poor career choice as it turned out. Naturally rebellious and inclined to pocket things that didn't belong to him, Spanbauer would spend more time in the brig than on active duty. He was given a dishonorable discharge in November 1959, and then returned to his hometown. Almost immediately thereafter, Oshkosh and its surrounds experienced an unprecedented crime wave.

In January 1960, someone broke into a home in Appleton, making off with several items, including a .22 handgun. The following night, a man wielding just such a weapon robbed a couple in their home in Neenah. A week later, a man matching David Spanbauer's description snatched a 13-year-old from her bed in Appleton. He tried to rape the girl. When she resisted, he clubbed her with the butt of his pistol and fled.

Then next victim would not be so lucky. On January 12, 1960, a man broke into a Winnebago County home, tied up a 16-year-old babysitter and raped her. When the girl's uncle returned unexpectedly, the intruder shot him in the face and fled. Miraculously, the man survived.

But that was just the prelude to a series of burglaries, rapes, and armed robberies committed across southeastern Wisconsin over the next month. Eventually, on February 16, 1960, the crime wave was ended when police picked up David Spanbauer in Sheboygan County. Charged initially with carrying a concealed weapon, Spanbauer cracked under questioning and confessed to a catalog of crimes, including rape, robbery and attempted murder. Aged just 19, he was sent away for 70 years.

Spanbauer would serve just twelve of those 70 years before being paroled in 1972. Thereafter, he made a token effort at going straight before temptation got the better of him. On August 11, 1972, he was driving along Highway 51 when he spotted a pretty 17-year-old hitchhiker. The girl said that she was on her way to her waitressing job, and Spanbauer promised to drive her. Instead, he took her to Token Creek Park, where he drew a knife and ordered her to strip. He then tied the girl up and raped her before driving away, leaving her stranded. Arrested soon after, the habitual criminal was sentenced to just 12 years, although in this case he'd serve every day of that prison time.

Walking free in 1991, Spanbauer landed a job at the Seven-Up bottling plant in Oshkosh and got himself an apartment. To all the world, it appeared that he had finally gotten his life together. But that, of course, was just a front. Almost immediately after his release, Spanbauer began trawling again, looking for houses to burgle and women to assault. Soon his criminal activities would veer in a far more sinister direction – toward murder.

On August 23, 1992, 10-year-old Ronelle Eichstedt was riding her bicycle near her home in Ripon when she disappeared without a trace. Her ravaged corpse would turn up six weeks later in a cornfield, 100 miles from where she had been taken. The little girl had been stabbed and strangled to death.

Almost two years later, on July 4, 1994, another cyclist had a terrifying encounter with a man driving a maroon Pontiac. Twenty-four-year-old Miriam Stariha was rear-ended hard enough to force her off the road. The driver then emerged from the car carrying a pistol, but he got back into his vehicle and sped off when another car approached.

Miriam Stariha was lucky. Others who encountered David Spanbauer during the summer of 1994 fared less well. On July 9, less than a week after he'd assaulted Miriam Stariha, Spanbauer broke into a home in Appleton and shot 21-year-old Trudi Jeschke to death. On Labor Day, September 5, he forced 12-year-old Cora Jones into his car, drove her 75 miles to Langlade County and there raped, stabbed and strangled her. Cora's body was found dumped in a ditch. On October 20, a 15-year-old girl was raped by a man who pulled her into his maroon Pontiac. On November 5, a 31-year-old woman suffered the same fate.

Then, on November 14, the police finally got a break in the case. Gerald Argall arrived at his home in Combined Locks, Wisconsin to find a man trying to break into the property. The burglar tried to flee, but Argall gave chase, tackled the man around the waist and held him until the police arrived.

The burglar, David Spanbauer, was taken into custody and subjected to intense interrogation. Eventually, after four days, he cracked and started talking. As investigators sat dumbstruck, he rattled off a barely believable list of rapes and burglaries ending with a confession to the murders of Ronelle Eichstedt, Trudi Jeschke, and Cora Jones.

Spanbauer would repeat his confession at trial, pleading guilty to some charges and no contest to others. He would end up with a jail term totaling 403 years, of which he'd only serve eight. David Spanbauer died of liver failure at Dodge Correctional Institution on July 29, 2002.

Frank Spisak Jr.

Frank G. Spisak Jr. is one of the most improbable serial killers you are likely to encounter. An avowed Nazi, he was also a cross-dressing transvestite who prostituted himself in a frizzy black wig and badly applied makeup. At other times he was known to dress up as Adolf Hitler and goose-step across his living room while listening to recordings of the Fuhrer's speeches.

It had not always been that way. At one stage, Spisak had been a history major at

Cleveland State University; at one stage he'd had a wife and a daughter and a normal job. Then, in 1976, Spisak suffered a head injury in an auto accident and his behavior took a turn for the bizarre. He started confiding to his wife, Laverne, his desire to become a woman. And his interest in the Third Reich, first nurtured during his school days, became an obsession. Eventually, Laverne departed, taking their daughter with her. Spisak was left alone in an empty apartment.

After Laverne left, Spisak started dressing as a woman full-time. He also started hormone treatments and began talking to a psychologist about a sex change operation. At the same time, his Hitler obsession reached new levels, and he started a new hobby, collecting guns and ammunition. Soon he would put those weapons to use.

On the morning of February 1, 1982, Spisak was at the Cleveland State University library reading a book about Nazi propaganda. At some point, he got up to use the bathroom. Also in the bathroom at the time was a black man, Reverend Horace Rickerson. When Rickerson walked into a stall, Spisak slid into the next cubicle, drew his gun and fired through the partition, emptying his clip. Rickerson was hit several times and died on the spot while Spisak walked calmly away from the scene.

The murder of Horace Rickerson thrilled Spisak. He wanted more. At the time, he was hanging with another Nazi wannabe, Ron Reddish. The pair began cruising the streets in Reddish's Buick LeSabre, looking for black men to attack. On a warm June night in 1982, they encountered factory worker John Hardaway on a deserted train station. Spisak fired at Hardaway, hitting him five times. Miraculously, Hardaway survived. The next two victims would not be so lucky.

On August 27, CSU handyman Tim Sheehan encountered Spisak in a bathroom on the university campus. Sheehan was standing at a urinal when Spisak attacked without warning, firing four shots into Sheehan's neck, head, and chest before fleeing. The next night, he went hunting again, gunning down 17-year-old Brian Warford at a bus shelter just outside the CSU campus.

Ballistics had by now confirmed to Cleveland PD that they had a serial shooter on their streets. But they had no idea who the perpetrator might be until September 4, when they caught an unexpected break in the case. An inebriated man was reported firing a pistol from the front window of his home. That man turned out to be Frank Spisak, and the weapon he was firing turned out to be the same one used in the CSU killings. Spisak had no problem admitting to the murders. In fact, he seemed proud of them.

By the time Spisak's court date came around, he had cultivated a Hitler mustache and bore a striking resemblance to the man he so idolized. He walked into court with a copy of Mein Kampf under his arm and greeted the judge with a snappy "Heil Hitler" salute. If that was an attempt to support his insanity defense, it failed. Found guilty of first-degree murder, Spisak was sentenced to death. It would take the State of Ohio nearly 30 years to carry out that sentence.

Frank Spisak Jr. was eventually put to death on February 17, 2011. In keeping with his rather unconventional life, his final words consisted of a five-minute reading from the Book of Revelations – in German. Then, as the drugs that would end his life began to flow, Spisak took a series of deep inhalations and made a snoring sound. He was pronounced dead ten minutes later.

William Suff

On October 30, 1986, the body of a young woman was found in an industrial area in Riverside, California. The victim, 23-year-old Michelle Gutierrez, was a known prostitute in the area. Now she was dead, stabbed in the face, chest, and buttocks by an unknown assailant and then strangled with a ligature. It was a tragedy, of course, but not an entirely unexpected one. Prostitution is, after all, a risky business.

Less than six weeks later, on December 11, another body was found, although in this case the corpse was so badly decomposed that it was impossible to determine cause of death. But then there was another dead woman, this one found in January 1987 along a stretch of road in Lake Elsinore. And then another, 27-year-old Martha Bess Young, found on May 2. Like the other victims, Young was a hooker, and the police by now had little doubt. There was a serial killer on the streets of Riverside.

But catching the perpetrator was going to be a difficult task, especially as he seemed to have the inside track on police activity. No sooner had the Riverside Police Chief announced the formation of a task force when the killer dropped out of sight. He would remain so for nearly two years.

Then, on January 27, 1989, he was back, killing 37-year-old Linda Mae Ruiz in bizarre fashion on a beach at Lake Elsinore. Ruiz was fed enough alcohol to make her pass out. Then the killer buried her head in the sand, causing her to asphyxiate.

The Riverside Prostitute Killer (as the press were calling him) returned to more conventional methods on June 28, 1989, battering 28-year-old Kimberly Lyttle to death and dumping her body in Cottonwood Canyon. But he'd been careless this time, leaving behind several fibers and pubic hairs which would later come back to haunt him. For now, though, he was still out there, still killing. On November 11, 1989, Judy Lynn Angel, 36, became his latest victim, and a month later 23-year-old Christina Leal joined the grim toll. Again, there were clues – tire tracks, pubic hairs, and fibers – but these got the police no closer to catching him.

On January 18, 1990, an early morning jogger stumbled upon the semi-nude body of a woman, later identified as 24-year-old Darla Jane Ferguson. Three weeks later, on February 8, farm workers found the nude body of 35-year-old prostitute Carol Lynn Miller. Eight months after that, a 33-year-old prostitute named Cheryl Coker was found in a Riverside industrial park, stabbed and strangled to death. She was soon followed by victim number 12, later identified as Susan Sternfeld.

There were three more murders between February and August before the police finally made some progress in the case. That was when a man driving a gray van picked up a prostitute near the University of California, took her to a quiet spot and then, without warning, began assaulting her. Fortunately, the woman was able to fight him off and escape, but she later saw the same man picking up another prostitute, 23-year-old Kelly Marie Hammond. Hammond's naked corpse was found later that evening.

The police now had a solid description of the suspect and his vehicle, and soon those details were being distributed by every media outlet in the area. But it did nothing to stop the carnage. If anything, it made the killer more brazen. Two more women died in September and October before the killer took an outrageous risk, dumping his nineteenth victim just a few blocks from the Riverside Police Station. She was 39-year-old Eleanore Casares, and she'd been strangled and stabbed. The killer had also hacked off her right breast, apparently carrying it away with him.

Nineteen women were now dead, and the police appeared powerless to stop the slaughter. Then, on the night of January 9, 1992, they caught a lucky break. Officers patrolling along University Avenue saw the driver of a gray van make an illegal U-turn and pulled him over. The man at the wheel identified himself as William Suff, and since he was driving with an expired license, the officers took him into custody. It was only back at the station that detectives realized that he was a perfect match for their suspect.

Checking into Suff's background, investigators learned that he had already served time for murder, after beating his two-year-old daughter to death back in 1974. He'd served just ten years for that heinous crime. Now, though, there was enough evidence to send him to Death Row. The results were back from the lab, and they linked him to several of the murder victims through fibers, pubic hairs and bodily fluids.

William Suff went on trial in March 1995. He entered not guilty pleas to all charges, but in truth, he never stood a chance, not with such overwhelming forensic evidence against him. Found guilty on 12 counts of murder, he was sentenced to death. He currently awaits execution at San Quentin State Prison.

Joseph Donald Ture Jr.

This wasn't a murder; this was a massacre. In the frigid early hours of December 15, 1978, someone broke into the house that single mom Alice Huling shared with her four children in a remote area of Stearns County, south of St. Cloud, Minnesota. The intruder was carrying a shotgun, and he proceeded to use it on the sleeping family, shooting Alice and three of her children – 16-year-old Susan; Wayne, 13; and Patti, aged 12 – to death. The fourth child, eleven-year-old Billy, was also shot at, but in the dark, the killer somehow managed to miss and Billy had the presence of mind to play dead. The man then fled the house, leaving behind a bloodbath. Despite the best efforts of police, the murders went unsolved. They would remain so for twenty years.

Some six months later, on May 8, 1979, Mary Wohlenhaus returned to her home in rural Afton, Minnesota and found her daughter, Marlys, lying on the basement floor in a pool of blood. Marlys was rushed to hospital where doctors performed emergency surgery in an effort to save her life. The injuries, however, were just too severe. The eighteen-year-old had been struck several times on the head with a hatchet, causing massive brain trauma and hemorrhaging. She died two days later, without ever regaining consciousness.

A reward of $50,000 was offered for the arrest and conviction of Marlys Wohlenhaus's killer. And at least there were clues this time. A neighbor had seen a van racing away from the Wohlenhaus residence at around 3:15 on the day in question. And a friend of Marlys came forward with an interesting story to tell. She said that she and Marlys had been at a restaurant in Afton on the day prior to the murder. Marlys had become upset after seeing a man watching them, a blonde-haired man in a leather coat, sunglasses and a baseball cap. Then, after the women left the restaurant, the man had followed them for some distance on his motorcycle. Did this suggest that Marlys had known her killer? The police thought so but ultimately came up empty after questioning Marlys's male acquaintances. This case, too, would go unsolved.

And that would have horrific consequences for several other young women. Shortly after the Wohlenhaus murder, there were a spate of abductions and rapes of young women in St. Paul, Minnesota. Many of the victims were waitresses, abducted from outside their places of work. One of them, 19-year-old waitress Diane Edwards, would end up shot to death. Shortly after that murder, the police arrested a 28-year-old mechanic named Joseph Ture, who had been seen hanging around a number of the abduction sites. In 1981, Ture was convicted of Diane Edwards's murder as well as numerous rapes. He was sentenced to life in prison.

In the early 1990s, a cold case investigator named Everett Doolittle was revisiting the Wohlenhaus murder when he got to hear of an inmate, currently serving time for murder, who had confessed to killing Marlys. The confession had, in fact, been submitted in writing back in 1981, but it had been dismissed by the authorities. The reason? Investigators had learned that Ture was working a shift at the Ford plant in St. Paul at the time Marlys was killed. Now Doolittle revisited that information and discovered a glaring error. It hadn't been Joe Ture pulling that shift on the production line, it had been his father, Joseph Ture Sr.

Doolittle now confronted Ture Jr. with his written confession, fully believing that he would admit the murder. To his surprise, Ture did the opposite. He now denied having anything to do it. He'd only made the confession, he said, because he'd wanted to be sent to the state mental hospital for treatment.

That was a setback, but fortunately for Doolittle, Ture (like most psychopaths) enjoyed boasting about his evil deeds. Over the years, he'd talked to several inmates about the murder, revealing details only the killer would have known. He'd also bragged about four other murders – the slaughter of the Huling family.

Almost 22 years after he murdered Marlys Wohlenhaus, Alice Huling and her children, Susan, Wayne, and Patti, Joseph Ture was brought before the courts to answer for his deeds. The Huling and Wohlenhaus trials were conducted separately, but the outcome was the same. Ture was found guilty. He was sentenced to a total of five life terms.

Gary Alan Walker

Eddie Cash was a man of regular habits. So when a neighbor didn't see him around their neighborhood in Broken Arrow, Oklahoma for a couple of days, she called the police. A cruiser was then sent to investigate, with the officers walking in on a scene of utter chaos. Eddie Cash lay dead on the floor in a pool of congealed blood, his face badly battered, an electrical cord still looped tightly around his neck. The house had also been ransacked and Eddie's 1976 Dodge truck was missing. An alert immediately went out for the vehicle.

By the time that alert was issued, however, Eddie Cash's Dodge was miles away, heading south towards Heavener, Oklahoma. The man at the wheel was a recently released felon named Gary Alan Walker, a diagnosed schizophrenic with a rap sheet dating back fifteen years and incorporating just about every crime on the statute book. Doctors had stressed that Walker was a danger to others and should remain behind bars, but an Oklahoma parole board had disagreed. They'd turned Walker loose in February

1984. Eddie Cash had already paid an appalling price for their mistake.

But Walker was only just getting started. In Heavener, he sold the Dodge for a few hundred bucks and then hitched a ride to Poteau. There, he struck up a conversation in a bar with a pretty 36-year-old named Margaret Bell. He convinced her to take him for a ride in her Caddy, then produced a knife and raped her. Margaret was then subjected to a prolonged ordeal, a road trip from hell during which she was forced to drive Walker to Arkansas, Tennessee and Kentucky. At every stop, she was savagely raped and sodomized, before Walker eventually tired of the game and strangled her to death, concealing her body in a haystack.

Walker next showed up in Vinita, Oklahoma, where he encountered Jane Hilburn watering her lawn on the morning of May 14. The "For Sale" sign planted outside the house provided him with the perfect way in. After persuading Jane to show him the property, he subjected the attractive 35-year-old to a torment of rape and sodomy. Then he strangled the unfortunate woman, loaded up her valuables and drove away in her black Camaro, heading south towards Tulsa on I-44.

The following day, Walker showed up in Oakhurst, Oklahoma where he tried to abduct an 18-year-old hitchhiker. The girl was lucky to escape. On May 20, he abducted a couple of 17-year-olds, then pushed the male out of the car and raced away with the terrified girl inside the vehicle. She would later be raped and forced to perform oral sex but would escape with her life after Walker fell asleep. The next victim would not be so lucky.

Aware that the police would now be searching for the Camaro, Walker abandoned it in an oilfield and then started walking towards Tulsa. Three days later, he snatched 32-year-old Janet Jewell from a busy street in broad daylight. Janet was driven to a remote location in her own car, then repeatedly raped at knifepoint before being strangled with a length of cord. Her body was later found in a creek in Okmulgee County.

By now, the Oklahoma State police had established a ring of roadblocks around Tulsa, hoping to catch the wild-haired man who had been described in the series of rapes and abductions. But Walker outfoxed them, avoiding the dragnet by remaining in town. And he was hardly lying low. On May 24, he abducted Valarie Shaw-Hartzell, a popular local news reporter, from the Towne West Shopping Mall. Valerie was taken to a rural road on the outskirts of Kellyville, where she was raped and sodomized several times during the night. The following morning, Walker drove her to a Tulsa drive-thru bank where he instructed her to cash a check for $650. Then he put her behind the wheel of her truck and told her to drive towards Claremore. There she endured another night of rape and sodomy before Walker strangled her to death the next morning.

On May 25, with half of the cops in Oklahoma looking for him, Walker drove into Tulsa and embarked on a drinking spree. Later that same night, he kidnapped a young woman in Vinita, holding her hostage for two days, raping her at will. Amazingly, the five-time killer let this victim go. He showed up next in Van Buren, Arkansas, where he committed a series of burglaries and tried to hold up a grocery store. He then abducted two women, one of them five months pregnant.

Here the case takes a decidedly strange turn. Rather than raping and killing his victims, Walker drove them around for a few hours before pawning his gun so that he could buy them lunch. He then gave them some money to take a bus home, even kissing one of the women on the cheek and telling her to take care. Then he stole a car and headed back to Tulsa, shacking up in a trailer park where he was arrested a few days later.

Gary Alan Walker would receive the ultimate penalty for the murder of his first victim, Eddie Cash. He was put to death by lethal injection on Thursday, January 13, 2000.

Frank Athen Walls

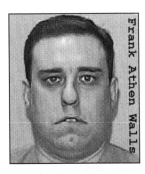

In the early hours of Wednesday, July 22, 1987, Edward Alger and his girlfriend Ann Peterson were asleep in their trailer in Okaloosa County, Florida, when they were awakened by a loud bang. Alger, an airman at the nearby Eglin Air Force Base, went to investigate and found himself confronted by a man holding a gun. The intruder instructed Alger to lie on the floor and then told Ann Peterson to tie his hands behind his back, bind his ankles and gag him. He then instructed the terrified young woman to lie down so that he could restrain her in the same manner. He was busy doing that when Alger managed to free himself.

The airman launched himself at the bulky intruder, knocking the gun from his hand. But the intruder had another weapon and now he drew it. A wicked blade flashed in the half light and bit deep into Edward Alger's throat. Still, the young man refused to give up the fight. Even as he fell, he gained a grip on his assailant's leg and sank his teeth in. The attacker had recovered his gun by now, however, and he was quick to use it. Three shots rang out, each of them delivering a bullet into Alger's head at close range. He was dead by the time he hit the floor. The intruder, whose original intent had been burglary, now turned his attention to Ann Peterson as she lay whimpering on the floor, trying to speak through the gag he'd placed in her mouth. Perhaps she was trying to beg for mercy. If so, her pleas fell on deaf ears. The intruder ripped off her clothes with the probable intention of raping her. Then, as she managed to loosen her gag and started screaming, he ended her life with two bullets to the head.

Edward Alger was usually a reliable young man and so, when he failed to show up for work the next day, his supervisor came looking for him. Sergeant John Calloway got no reply when he knocked on the door, so he entered, walking in on a bloodbath. Soon the trailer park was crawling with detectives and crime scene technicians. They'd barely got to work when a call came in telling them to check out a 19-year-old man named Frank Walls. Officers then carried out a raid on Walls's residence and uncovered enough evidence to arrest him for the double homicide.

Those murders, as it turned out, were just the tip of the iceberg. Investigators soon got a DNA match, linking Walls to the bloody slaying of 47-year-old Audrey Gygi, a month earlier. Gygi had been raped and then stabbed to death in her trailer, a stone's throw away from the one where Alger and Peterson had been killed. The killer had left behind a semen stain on the bed sheet, and it was through that stain that investigators were now able to link the crime to Walls.

There were other murders, too. Nineteen-year-old Tommie Lou Whiddon had been attacked as she lay sunbathing on Okaloosa Island on March 26, 1985. The young woman's throat had been so deeply slashed that she was almost decapitated. And then there was Cynthia Sue Condra, 24 years old on the day in September 1986 when her body was dumped near Lewis Turner Boulevard in Wright, Florida. She had been stabbed 21 times.

Walls made only a cursory attempt at denying these murders before he broke down and admitted his guilt. He blamed his "uncontrollable urge to kill," and that would be a theme picked up by his defense team at trial. They argued that their client had been diagnosed as bipolar during his teens and had been on anti-psychotic medication. However, that defense was blown out of the water when a female prison officer testified that Walls had told her he was faking mental illness in order to avoid the death penalty.

Frank Walls was found guilty of all five murders and received life terms for four of them. For the murder of Ann Peterson, however, he was sentenced to die by lethal injection.

But Walls's attorneys were not about to go down without a fight. In 1991, they launched an appeal arguing that the trial judge should not have allowed the corrections officer's testimony. And the Florida Supreme Court agreed, overturning the conviction.

The victory, however, would be of short duration. In 1992, Walls was re-tried, again found guilty, and again sentenced to death. He currently awaits execution.

Lesley Eugene Warren

Lesley Warren was reasonably good-looking and he was a smooth talker, the kind of man, in other words, who had little problem picking up women. But those who fell for the Fort Drum soldier's charms usually had cause to regret it before very long. Patsy Vineyard discovered that to her cost on May 20, 1987. Patsy's husband, Michael, was also a Fort Drum soldier. But he was away on that Wednesday night when Patsy met Lesley Warren at a bar and agreed to go with him to an abandoned barracks on the base. The following day, Private Vineyard returned to find his wife missing. Her strangled corpse was discovered days later, floating in the Black River near Sackets Harbor, New York. She was just the first of eight women who would die at the hands of the so-called "Baby-faced Killer."

Lesley Eugene Warren was born in Chandler, North Carolina on October 15, 1967. He endured a difficult childhood during which he was physically and psychologically abused by his father. At the same time, his younger brother, Laron, was idolized by both parents, leading to Lesley becoming increasingly withdrawn. That continued until his parents divorced in 1973, with Lesley's mother getting custody of the children. But the damage had already been done. Despite his obvious intelligence, Lesley was no more than an average student at school, and he'd eventually be expelled without graduating. By then, he was already well-known to local law enforcement, having been arrested on a catalog of charges ranging from drug possession to rape.

In October 1986, Lesley gave in to his mother's cajoling and enlisted in the U.S. Army. Perhaps Phyllis Warren thought that military life would settle her son down, but it appeared to have the opposite effect. He continued committing petty crimes and, within six months of enlisting, had committed his first murder, that of Patsy Vineyard. Soon after, he went AWOL from Fort Bragg and was flagged as a deserter and given a dishonorable discharge.

Warren returned to his hometown of Chandler, North Carolina. There, he enrolled on a three-month truck driver course and eventually landed a job with AM-CAN Haulage Company. That, of course, provided the perfect cover. The murder of Patsy Vineyard had left him with an appetite for more, and in the summer of 1989, he struck again, picking up a woman in Tennessee, strangling her to death and dumping her corpse in a forest.

On August 26, 1989, Warren was driving his rig when he came upon 42-year-old Velma Faye Gray, standing beside her wrecked car. Playing the knight in shining armor, he offered the woman a ride, then beat and strangled her to death before dumping her body at Lake Bowen in South Carolina. That was followed in May

1990 by the strangulation of 39-year-old Jayme Hurley, who had made the grave mistake of giving Warren her phone number.

Killing someone he knew, however, turned out to be a grave mistake. Warren was pulled in for questioning and later arrested after Hurley's purse was found in his truck. Then, while he was out on bail, his mother called the police and implicated him in the murder of Patsy Vineyard.

With the police now alerted to him as a potential serial killer, Warren went on the run. But he was hardly lying low. On July 15, 1990, he picked up 21-year-old Katherine Johnson and took her to a motel where they had consensual sex. He then strangled her to death. Johnson's body was later found in the trunk of a car parked on the motel's lot.

On July 17, the police issued a nationwide alert for Lesley Warren. The following day, Warren's brother came forward to reveal that Warren had confided the location of Jayme Hurley's corpse. The decomposed remains were disinterred from their shallow grave that same day. Within hours of this gruesome discovery, Lesley Warren would be in custody.

Warren was subjected to a fierce round of interrogation. He eventually cracked and confessed to the murders of Patsy Vineyard, Velma Gray, Jayme Hurley and Katherine Johnson, adding nonchalantly that he'd actually killed eight women but couldn't remember the names of the other four.

The four that he did remember, however, proved enough. Convicted in North Carolina for the murder of Jayme Hurley, Warren was sentenced to death, that sentence upheld by both the North Carolina and US Supreme Courts. The "Baby-faced Killer" currently awaits execution.

Richard Paul White

Perhaps it was the threat of the death penalty that got Richard Paul White talking, perhaps it was the need to unburden himself of his horrible crimes. White had been arrested at his home in Denver, Colorado on September 9, 2013, and had been booked for the murder of a co-worker, 27-year-old Jason Reichardt. He had offered a highly improbable explanation for the shooting, one that his interrogators refused to accept.

According to White, he'd been demonstrating the safety features of his 9mm pistol to Reichardt, trying to prove to him that the weapon would not fire while the safety was engaged. But the very feature that White had been trying to demonstrate had not been engaged. He'd pulled the trigger and the gun had discharged, hitting Reichardt in the face and killing him instantly. "We don't believe that and neither will a jury," one of the detectives told him. "So you'd better start telling the truth while you've still got some options available to you."

White had mulled that over for several hours before asking to speak to the detectives again. But to their surprise, he didn't want to speak about the Reichardt shooting. "What if I was to tell you that I could clear up some unsolved homicides for you?" he suggested.

"Can you?" one of the detectives asked.

"Depends what's on the table," White replied coyly.

And so a deal was struck, with White promising to come clean on three murders in exchange for immunity from capital punishment. He delivered on two of those cases almost immediately, directing officers to the backyard of his home at 2885 Albion Street and pointing out two areas for them to start digging. Before long, they had unearthed the remains of two women, later identified as Annaletia Maria Gonzales, 27, and Victoria Lyn Turpin, 32. According to White, both of the women were prostitutes who he had picked up on Colfax Avenue, a 26-mile-long stretch that runs straight through the metropolitan area and is a popular place of business for hookers and drug dealers. He'd taken the women home where he'd held them captive for several hours, raping and sexually torturing them until he'd had his fill of depravity. Then he'd taken a belt and strangled them to death before burying them in the yard.

The third victim had not been picked up on Colfax and was not a prostitute. White said that he'd spotted her standing at a bus stop and had offered her a ride. "The minute I saw her," he said, "I knew I had to have her." He then pointed to a tattoo of a Native American maiden on his forearm. "That's because I had this picture of her on my skin all this time."

This unfortunate woman had been taken back to White's house where she had suffered the same fate as the others. However, she had not been buried in the backyard. Instead, White had driven her corpse to the small town of Mesita, some 240 miles south of Denver. White had grown up in this tiny community and his father still lived there. His victim had been committed to a sandy grave on the outskirts of town. Now White pointed out the spot, and a couple of police officers started digging, finding the decomposing remains just a few feet below the surface. She was Torrey Marie Foster, a 25-year-old mother of two who had disappeared in 2002.

White had now confessed to the sex slayings of three women, but he wasn't done yet. He said that he had killed five more women, burying three of them at locations around the state and throwing the other two bodies into a river in Otero County. None of those bodies was ever found and White has never been charged.

He was, however, indicted for the murders of Annaletia Maria Gonzales, Victoria Lyn Turpin and Jason Reichardt, pleading guilty at trial and accepting a sentence of life in prison without parole. An additional 144 years were added on for the rape and torture of three more women who had survived his deadly intentions. Charges for the murder of Torrey Marie Foster will probably never be filed since White will remain behind bars for the rest of his natural life.